6

PEOPLE AND PLANET

EDITOR
TOM WOODHOUSE

People and Planet

The Right Livelihood Award Speeches

GREEN BOOKS

© Right Livelihood Foundation, 1987

First published by
Green Books
Hartland
Bideford
Devon EX39 6EE

Illustrations: Barbara Johnson
Cover: Simon Willby

British Library Cataloguing in Publication Data
People and Planet: Alternative Nobel Prize Speeches
1. Environmental Protection
I. Woodhouse, Tom
333. 7'2 TD170

ISBN 1 870098 02 1

Typeset by KMA Typesetting
70 The Square, Hartland
Printed by Robert Hartnoll (1985) Ltd.
Victoria Square, Bodmin, Cornwall

Contents

Preface
Foreword

CHAPTER ONE · The Rights of the Earth   3
Amory and Hunter Lovins · *Building Real Security*   10
Petra Kelly · *The Green Movement*   22
Wangari Maathai · *The Green Belt Movement in Kenya*   33
Duna Kor · *The Environment in Eastern Europe*   46
Chief Ibedul Yataka Gibbons · *Nuclear Free Zone in Palau*   52

CHAPTER TWO · People's Economics   59
Leopold Kohr · *Over Development*   63
Manfred Max-Neef · *Barefoot Economics*   75
Cary Fowler and Pat Mooney · *Agricultural Heritage*   84
Leif Sandholt · *Western Affluence and Third World Poverty*   94

CHAPTER THREE · The Cooperative Community   101
S. Tilakaratna · *Rural Development*   107
Ela Bhatt · *Women's Development in India*   114
Stephen Gaskin · *International Aid*   119
Anwar Fazal · *The Consumer Movement*   124

CHAPTER FOUR · Human Centered Technology   133
Mike Cooley · *Lucas and Socially Useful Production*   138
Bill Mollison · *Permanent Agriculture*   154
Dr. Hassan Fathy · *People's Architecture*   159

CHAPTER FIVE · The Rights of People   169
Theodoor van Boven · *Human Rights*   176
Winefreda Estanero-Geonzon · *The Rights of Prisoners*   184
Rajni Kothari · *Grassroots Development*   191
Iman Khalife · *Peace in Lebanon*   201
Sir George Trevelyan · *Spiritual Education*   207
Patrick van Rensburg · *Education for Social Change*   214

I wish to acknowledge the help of Vithal Rajan who provided valuable guidance in preparing this book; to Geoffrey Redfearn and Bernard Stinson and to Satish Kumar and Julia Meiklejohn of Green Books.

Tom Woodhouse

To those who have supported the work
of the Right Livelihood Foundation.

Preface

The concept of right livelihood comes from the eight-fold path, the middle way, ennunciated by the Buddha in the sixth century before Christ. Lately, it has been recommended as a way of life by Schumacher to avoid the perils of over-industrialisation. From historical times, great civilizations have risen and fallen in their pursuit of power and wealth. The wheel of life, which turning leads to the grandest of human achievements, seems also to plunge us into the darkest of our tragedies. A life of moderation, of simplicity and peace, of love for one another, of respect for all Creation, and of harmony with nature is a way out of this cycle of triumph and tragedy. The message is as relevant today as during the days of the Buddha.

The disaster at Chernobyl underlines our fears for the environment of our poisoned and plundered planet. The threat of nuclear war and destruction of all life on earth has increased with the passing years since Hiroshima. The world, even with the speediest family planning measures, will reach a total population of about fifteen billion people in the 21st century. Great as are these threats to our survival, they are not the top concerns of the great majority of the human race, who are very poor and who live in the Third World. They are threatened by poverty itself, by lack of social justice, and by the technological domination of the West.

If the varying interests of the haves and the have-nots, of the several nations and ethnic groups in conflict, are to be resolved without catastrophic collapse, if humanity is to achieve the beatific visions of saints and scholars, of poets and scientists, a middle way has to be found between these confrontations. The Right Livelihood Awards recognize this need, and its winners are the symbols of this search. There are no losers, for the point is to see that humanity does not lose.

Vithal Rajan
Executive Director of the Foundation
November 1986

Foreword

The Right Livelihood Award, which has become known as the 'Alternative Nobel Prize', aims to strengthen 'alternative' experiments, projects which provide practical and replicable solutions to the dangers we face. The awards give financial support as well as encouragement, publicity and protection. In 1979, I asked the Nobel Foundation to consider the creation of a new award for work aimed specifically at meeting the needs of the Third World and of our planet. When my proposal was not accepted, I decided to create and endow such an award myself. With the help of donations from an international network of friends, the award is now self-financing at its present level of US$100,000 p.a. Several recipients share the award money which goes to the projects and is not for personal use. Since 1982, an Honorary Award is also presented to persons or projects not primarily in need of money, but likely to benefit from the publicity attached to the award. Anybody can nominate a person or project (except their own) for the Right Livelihood Award. The nominations are presented to an international jury whose members work in an honorary capacity and decide by consensus. The composition of the jury varies in order to incorporate as broad a spectrum of opinion as possible. Past and present members include:

— H. E. Rodrigo Carazo, former President of Costa Rica and founder president of the UN University for Peace.
— Ambassador James George
  Member of the UN Disarmament Commission.
— Birgitta Hambraeus
  Member of the Swedish Parliament.
— Sven Hamrell
  Director of the Dag Hammarskjold Foundation.
— Thor Heyerdahl
  Explorer and writer
— Robert Muller
  former Assistant Secretary-General of the United Nations.

- Michaela Walsh
  President of Women's World Banking
- Ponna Wignaraja
  former Secretary-General of the Society for International Development.
- Monika Griefahn
  Greenpeace

The Right Livelihood Award ceremony has been held annually since 1980 in Stockholm on December 9th—the day before the Nobel Prize presentations—and since 1985 takes place in the Swedish Parliament. Award winners cover a wide spectrum, both geographically and as regards their work. The award serves to create coalitions and networks between groups who had hitherto often been unaware of each other.

At the award ceremony in 1982, the Asian consumer protection activist, Anwar Fazal, met the British mystic and 'educator of the adult spirit', Sir George Trevelyan. Out of their mutual respect grew an alliance in their common struggle against unscrupulous materialism, which is responsible for both the spiritual sterility of the consumer society and the profit-hungry exploitation of the Third World. These new coalitions give hope. We cannot separate the search for peace in the world, for peace with nature and for peace within ourselves. Together with our allies in the Third World, who are not susceptible to the illusions of the throw-away society, we must save this planet from war, destruction and delusion. We must not expect answers from politicians who have chosen to remain in the concrete towers of their obsolete thinking and are afraid of our attempts to free them from their ideological prisons.

Whether we succeed, whether we can promote our solutions widely and effectively enough in the short time left to change course, remains an open question. But as long as it does remain open we must do our best and be prepared to risk everything, for it is indeed a question of all or nothing, of the survival of mankind and the living earth. Will we meet the challenge or will the great opportunity encounter too small a people? We are living in an era in which, as E. F. Schumacher said, it is fashionable to be sceptical about everything which makes demands on us. Would it not be better to be sceptical about this very scepticism, which makes no demands on us at all?

Here are examples of what so-called ordinary people can do to bring about positive change. The aim of this book is to encourage you, dear reader, to follow in their footsteps to begin implementing your vision, to 'walk your talk', as the Native Americans say. For if not now, then when? And if not you, then who?

Jakob von Uexkull
August 1986

Requests for further information about the work of the Foundation, and nominations for an Award, should be directed to:
The Research Fellow, Right Livelihood Awards Foundation, School of Peace Studies, University of Bradford, Bradford, West Yorkshire, BD7 1DP, United Kingdom.
Tel 0274 733466

CHAPTER ONE

The Rights of The Earth

The Rights of The Earth

"The Right Livelihood Award aims to help the West find a wisdom to match its science, and the Third World to find a science to match its ancient wisdom"
Jakob von Uexkull, Introductory Speech 1984

THERE has been a tremendous upsurge of concern for the well-being of the planet, threatened as it is by the escalation of the nuclear and conventional arms race; by the continued extension of large scale industrialisation, with an attendant technology which is rapacious and polluting; and by the entrenchment of cynical and manipulative political and bureaucratic authorities which frequently seem to disregard human rights and human needs. Yet around the world people are confronting and creatively transcending the perils posed by such apparently insuperable forces. Drawing on traditional wisdoms, cultures, and techniques, on the creativity, imagination, and courage inherent in the human spirit, people are building alternatives to the methods of the military-industrial megamachine.

In Western Europe the Green parties have emerged to present a persuasive critique of the values of industrialism, and the need to develop practical policies to deal with the crisis of industrialism and militarism within a global perspective: "The industrialised countries can attain a new relationship with the countries of the Third World only if they renounce their continuous industrial expansion. We emphatically oppose the definition of 'development' simply as economic growth, at the expense of irreplaceable natural and cultural capital. This model of development, together with so-called development aid, leads the Third World countries to being exploited by the industrialised countries, and robbed of their own form of life and resources. In its place we shall try to develop jointly with the Third World countries those new ecological practices which will preserve us from becoming victims of the gathering world crisis" (1)

Changing the structure of economic relationships is linked to the objective of turning back the forces of militarism. Thus, from the UK Greens, "In the more decentralised society that we envisage, we shall be able to reduce our dependence on military power and develop nonviolent means of defence . . . ". The Greens, in short, have unambiguously developed a postion against the nuclear state, and the contribution of Petra Kelly and the Green Party in the Federal Republic of Germany has been of special significance. This point is illustrated clearly in Petra Kelly's speech, and the award was made to her because of the unique contribution she has made in the formation and the continued work of Die Grunen. Jakob von Uexkull recognised the exceptional degree of her commitment: "How many people have entered the hectic and exhausting political arena because they see themselves as representing not just their voters, not only the minorities, the ill and the socially weak—but the children, the coming generations, the animals and the plants as well? This is the task which Petra Kelly has taken upon herself. Extraordinary dangers demand extraordinary efforts, and I know of no one who devotes more effort to open up the sterile fossils of the institutions controlling our lives." (2)

Amory and Hunter Lovins have been amongst the most important advocates in the United States for a sustainable energy policy. They have made an impact both through their writings, and through the development of soft energy systems which work in practice. Much of their work is done through the Rocky Mountain Institute, a foundation established to promote efficient energy resource use and global security. The Lovins emphasise in their work the connection between high consumption (and especially nuclear) energy systems, and military insecurity: "We've worked on security issues for years . . . trying to stop the spread of nuclear bombs and to make the energy system more resilient, but we've also come to re-examine what makes people feel secure. It seems to be things that touch their lives directly, like having reliable and affordable necessities, a healthful environment, a sustainable economy, a cohesive society, a legitimate system of self government, and so on." (3). This point is elaborated with great clarity in their speech, 'Building Real Security'.

In the meantime, however, the superpowers do attempt to coerce smaller peoples into compliance with their wishes. Small countries also resist, and this is amply illustrated in the struggle of the Palauns, the people of the Pacific whose desire to live in their land free of nuclear weapons has not been respected by the United States of America. The Republic of Palau in the western Pacific was the first nation in the world to adopt a Constitution banning the storage, testing and dumping of nuclear materials within its territory, unless the approval of 75% of the population is given in a referendum. A Compact of Free Association agreed by Palau and the US government representatives in 1982 grants Palau $1 billion in aid, and a form of self government (Palau was made a UN Strategic Trust Territory and placed under US administration in 1947). In return, the USA has demanded effective military authority over the islands, with an option to use up to one third of the land area for military bases and for the transit of vessels and aircraft carrying nuclear weapons.

This demand directly contradicts the Palauan constitution against nuclear weapons. In 1979 the Palauans approved their constitution by a 92% vote in favour, and reaffirmed their support for the nuclear free provisions in the constitution in two separate referenda (by majorities of 70% and 78%). Then in 1983, the people of Palau were asked to vote on the Compact of Free Association. The ballot asked them whether they would approve section 314 of the Compact, which would allow the USA to base nuclear weapons and nuclear powered ships on Palau. According to the Constitution, a 75% majority was needed to allow this to happen; in the event 53% voted in favour, well short of the required majority. In a separate question, a majority of the Palauans (62%) did vote in favour of the Compact of Free Association. However, for the Compact to take effect, it was a condition of the plebiscite that section 314 (the pro-nuclear clause) should also be accepted. Since this clearly was not passed by the required majority, the Compact could not take effect and the political status of Palau remains undecided. The Council of Chiefs and the High Chief Ibedul (the traditional leaders of the islanders) declared the Compact void, a position confirmed by a judgement of the Palau Supreme Court. The US State Department seems to insist that the majority in favour of the Compact be respected, and that the islanders will have to find a means of abandoning their nuclear free commitments, to allow the self government and financial assistance planned under the Compact to go ahead. In other words, the rights to self government and the prospects of US financial support are conditional on the revoking of the nuclear free element of the Constitution, and the granting to the US of military sovereignty over the island. At the same time there have been allegations of undue US interference in the organisation of the plebiscite, and the wording of the proposals put to the Palauan people. The prospect of the presence of America military bases on the island attracted the interests of Japanese industrial and commercial consortia, who developed plans for a superport, for an oil refinery and oil storage facility. At this point military and industrial interests combined.

But significant opposition to the superport, as well as to the military bases, developed among the Palauan people. In June 1986 President Remeliik was murdered in the street. Remeliik was for the Compact, but also in favour of the Constitution (requiring a 75% majority to allow nuclear use). He was replaced by Lazarus Salii, the most pro-US candidate. In January 1986, a revised version of the Compact was signed by the government, submitted in haste to the people, and still failed (in a referendum of February 1986) to overturn by the required majority the objections to the pro-nuclear clauses. It is now claimed by the Palau and US governments that the Compact conforms to the Palauan Constitution, despite the fact that section 314 allows the US to operate nuclear capable vessels and aircraft within Palau, and allows also for rights of virtually perpetual transit.

Opposition amongst the people continues, and in the struggle to maintain an effective nuclear free constitution, High Chief Ibedul Gibbons has played an important part. His speech presents a clear account of the desires of the Palauan people to remain nuclear free, a desire especially poignant coming as it does from the peoples of the Pacific who have, since the Second World War, already suffered the consequences of a series of nuclear weapons explosions in the tests carried out by western powers.

Peace is at risk most obviously from the threats made by the nuclear powers in the deployment of their weapons throughout the lands and oceans of the world. It is also at risk from the more insidious process of excessive exploitation of the earth and its resources. People have a need to live within a system of secure international relations founded on trust and mutuality, not on fear of annihilation. They also have a right to live in secure habitats. The Green Belt Movement in Kenya and the Duna Kor (Danube Circle) Group in Hungary have made this their concern. "Since 1984 when we (The Kenyan Green Belt Movement) received the award from the Right Livelihood Foundation, we have come a long way. We were talking then of some sixty nurseries, now we have about six hundred tree nurseries". (4)

The Green Belt Movement is a community tree planting project, conceived by Wangari Maathi in 1974, and adopted as a project of the National Council of Kenyan Women in 1977. The project was designed to approach the problem of development holistically, that is it aims to fulfil a range of social, cultural, political and economic needs as well as to cope with the technical problems of deforestation. Kenya has a population of 17 million, 90% of whom live in the rural areas where there is a great pressure on land and food supplies. For the vast majority of the population the main source of energy needs comes from wood fuel, and Kenya's forest cover has been reduced to less than 3%. At the same time, 35% of the country's foreign exchange is spent on the purchase of oil to fuel the city based industries which occupy 10% of the population. The story of how the Green Belt Movement responded to the problems resulting from this situation is lucidly told in the speech of Wangari Maathi. "The struggle to preserve our environment, to ensure that development does not remain a password for destruction, is now global. For a while we were told that countries which did not know the unfettered pursuit of private profit, would find it easier to preserve a healthy environment. Recent news from Eastern Europe shows that this is unfortunately not so." (5)

The people of Duna Kor in Hungary face a problem of a different order from that faced by the Green Belt Movement in Kenya. In this case, a large scale high technology project for the construction of a hydroelectric power plant threatens the environment of thousands of people. The Hungarian and Czechoslovakian governments jointly have planned the construction of a power plant at Nagymaros-Gabcikova on the Hungarian-Czechoslovakian border. The project involves the construction of two dams, and the rerouting of the course of the River Danube in a manner which will threaten a large part of northern Hungary with the loss of agricultural land, of animal habitats, of forests, and of irrigation and drinking water. The Duna Kor Group have emerged to oppose the project, combining in a unique fashion in Eastern Europe the struggle to protect the environment, with the struggle for political participation. The Hungarian government has banned the Duna Kor from registering as a legally recognised organisation, and its statements have been ignored in the official media, while its leaders have been obstructed and harassed. Nevertheless, dissident intellectuals and a wide variety of social groups in Hungary have participated in the organisation of a petition protesting against the project, and calling for a national referendum.

The speeches which follow in this section present a testimony to the global concern for a secure environment which unites north and south, east and west.

NOTES:
(1) Statement of Die Grunen, the German Green Party.
(2) Jakob von Uexkull, Introductory Speech, 1982.
(3) Quoted in Mother Earth News, July/August, 1984.
(4) Wangari Maathai in an interview with Joshua Mailman, President of the US Friends of the Right Livelihood Foundation.
(5) Jakob von Uexkull, Introductory Speech 1985.

BUILDING REAL SECURITY

Amory and Hunter Lovins

9th December 1983

THE GREAT challenge facing the world is to enable people to feel more safe, valued, empowered, and responsible: in short, to begin building real security through individual and community action. This motive underlay our work on least-cost, nonviolent energy strategies, and on how an economically rational energy policy can help to solve problems as diverse as CO_2-related climatic change, the lack of affordable energy for economic and cultural development, and the spread of nuclear bombs.

Four years ago we made a pilgrimage to the Peace Museum at Hiroshima. There we saw bones which the fires had fused into roof tiles, and granite steps which the flash of the bomb had changed into a different mineral form—except in one place where a person sitting on the steps had left a shadow in the stone.

Today, the nuclear bombs in the world are equivalent to more than one and a half million Hiroshimas, increasing by dozens per day. A single Poseidon submarine can carry about enough warheads to land the equivalent of three Hiroshimas on each of the 200-odd Soviet cities of over 100,000 people. The United States has 31 such submarines. Yet, apparently thinking these too few, the U.S. is also building bigger submarines, with Trident missiles accurate enough to attack Soviet missile silos—and why attack silos whose missiles have already been launched? Having decided that its thousand-odd land-based missiles are becoming more vulnerable to attack, the U.S. is building more of them: MX missiles, which have been trying for some fifteen years to find a hole to crawl into. The MX, with ten highly accurate warheads, is also a first-strike weapon, offering a bonus to the side that launches first. Soviet missile designs and policies appear to be moving in the same ominous direction, playing catch-up as they have done ever since 1945.

While American officials complain that arms-control treaties are hard to verify, U.S. actions seek to make them impossible to verify—by arming planes, ships, and perhaps pickup trucks with miniature, easily concealed cruise missiles. Similar missiles will doubtless soon appear on Soviet submarines. And while U.S. commentators shudder at the trigger-happiness of the Soviet command that decided, after more than two hours' deliberation, to shoot down a Korean airliner, President Reagan presses ahead with European siting of Pershing II misiles which will give that same Soviet command about six minutes to decide whether to blow up the world.

The Soviet government has offered to reduce its SS-20 missiles targeted on Western Europe to a level (some 120-140 missiles) amounting to about half the warheads, with less than a tenth of the explosive power, already targeted on Western Europe for the past two decades. By rejecting this offer, the United States has achieved no such reductions; on the contrary, there will now be hundreds of additional missiles on both sides—all probably on a hairtrigger "launch-on-warning" alert in which a malfunctioning 10-kronor computer chip could undo the evolutionary progress of the past few milliard years. And as a bonus added to this insanity, the Reagan Administration has also achieved in Western Europe what the Soviet Union could never accomplish: the popular delegitimation of NATO.

Since all these things are being done in the name of U.S.

national security, it is worth recalling a key insight which Philip Morrison and the Boston Study Group provided in their remarkable book 'The Price of Defense' (New York Times Book Co., 1979). They showed that there is no significant military threat to the United States that can be defended against. By this they meant that, owing to geography, Americans need not be worried about armadas of Soviets or Chinese in rowboats. Both are simply too far away to pose a conventional military threat to the North American landmass. Such threats could exist, and are of three kinds:

- terrorism—which a free society cannot defend against, though it could make itself less vulnerable and less tense;
- minor border incursions of the sort that the Coast Guard is designed to cope with; and
- strategic nuclear attack—against which there is no defense, although if one believes in deterrence one might be able to deter it. (Deterrence requires, among other paradoxical things, that each side be rational enough to be in fact deterred by the threat of mutual annihilation, yet also appear to the other side to be irrational enough to carry out that threat.)

The military threats of terrorism, border incursions, and nuclear attack, insofar as they can handled at all, can be handled (as the Boston Study Group's analysis showed) with military forces less than 3% the size and cost of present U.S. forces: in essence, by a Coast Guard plus a handful of Poseidon submarines. The other 97% of U.S. military budgets goes for general purpose forces to project American power into other people's disputes in other countries where the President of the United States perceives the U.S. has an interest (to put it as neutrally as we can).

For both the announced purpose of defense, and the unannounced purpose of bullying, the United States alone is spending about ten thousand dollars per second on more and allegedly better tools for killing people. World military expenditures are several times this level. But what sort of security is such military investment actually buying? In 1945, the United States was militarily all but invulnerable. Today, 30,000 bombs richer, the same nation is entirely exposed to devastation at any moment. Whatever that military budget is buying, it's not making Americans (or anyone else) really secure.

Indeed, security is being eroded, not only by the multiplication and refinement of weapons, but also by their spread. Nowadays the total firepower of World War II can be packaged to fit neatly beneath your bed. Nuclear delivery vehicles can thus include not just missiles, whose radar tracks mark their origin for retaliation, but also tramp freighters, fishing boats, ox carts, rental vans, and parcel services. If the middle of New York disappeared in a bright flash at 8.00 tomorrow morning, but nobody said "We did it," against whom would those "deterrent" missiles be launched? Nuclear attacks can be anonymous and thus undeterrable. As the seeds of nuclear bombs, sown for decades around the world, begin to germinate—so far in India, Israel, South Africa, Pakistan, and Argentina, and soon in such places as Iraq, Iran, Libya, Taiwan, South Korea, and Brazil—anonymous nuclear attacks become not only possible but likely. Military might cannot prevent such attacks and may even invite them.

The spread of nuclear bombs is motivated by the prestige attached to them and by the domineering capacity derived from them—notably by the United States, which is the only nation to have used them in anger, the only one which refuses to promise not to use them first again, and the main one basing its foreign policy on threats of nuclear violence (such threats having been made, on average, about once a year since 1945). These political ends are so inviting that only one country, Sweden, is known to have abandoned a bomb program already in progress (though she has apparently retained the means to make bombs quickly if she so chose).

Of course, making bombs requires not only motives but also means; and nuclear power programs have exported those means around the world. The materials, knowledge, skills, equipment, and organizations used for nuclear power are so unavoidably usable for bombs that it is impossible to have one without the other—notwithstanding efforts (notably by some distinguished Swedes) towards unachieveable "international safeguards". In contrast, in a world without nuclear power, the means needed to make bombs by any known method would no longer be items of commerce. They would therefore be hard to get, conspicuous to try to get, and politically very costly to be caught trying to get, because for the first time one's purpose in wanting them would be unambiguously military. This would make proliferation not impossible, but extremely difficult.

What stands in the way is the unwillingness of nuclear bureaucracies (and of the governments they often control) to abandon their hope of profit and personal satisfaction—neither of which has materialized—from subsidised exports of nuclear technology, notably to developing countries. In fact, nuclear power is dying of an incurable attack of market forces throughout the world's market economies. New plants are so uneconomic that even if built, they would cost less to write off (and buy energy efficiency instead) than to operate. Indeed, it can easily cost a nuclear utility more to build the capacity to serve a new, electrically heated building than it costs to construct that entire building!

Simply choosing the cheapest energy options can guarantee a non-nuclear future, regardless of personal preference or ideology. This is already starting to happen. Since 1979, for example, the United States has gotten more than a hundred times as much new energy from savings as from all expansions of energy supply; more new supply from renewable sources than from nonrenewables; and more new electric generating capacity ordered from small hydro plants and windpower than from coal or nuclear plants or both. (No large power plants of any kind have been ordered in the U.S. since late 1981; and the nuclear program, the world's largest, still delivers only about half as much energy as wood.) Yet successive U.S. Presidents have ignored these market realities and instead propped up tottering nuclear programs abroad by the bad example of their domestic energy policies. By saying that even a rich, skilful nation, rich in all sorts of fuels, cannot survive without nuclear power and a plutonium economy, the U.S. has reinforced similar arguments in other countries lacking those advantages. If the U.S. were simply to accept the verdict of the market, abstain from heroic measures to resuscitate a failed technology, design an orderly terminal phase for it, help a very imperfect market to work better in choosing cheaper alternatives, and help any other interested country to follow that good example, the world's remaining nuclear power programs—all in serious trouble— would soon wither.

The Swedish example in pioneering this sensible course is of critical worldwide importance for nonproliferation. A modern, highly industrialized country with no fossil fuels of its own has set out to abandon nuclear power by 2010 in favour of very efficient energy use and appropriate renewable sources: just the options which will save the most oil soonest and cheapest. Sweden's success in continuing to move in this direction will be a vital beacon showing other countries the way, just as the efficiency of using energy in Sweden today— probably the world's highest—is the universally cited example of what can be done by a cost-conscious and practical people. But the global nuclear industry so fears the persuasive power of the Swedish example that it has mis-represented the result of the referendum as a resounding endorsement of the nuclear future. Sweden's greatest contribution yet to world peace could be simply to proclaim what actually happened—that 78% of Swedish votes were for phasing out nuclear power in favour of alternatives—and to reinforce the national commitment to making that shift a model of smooth and efficient management.

That commitment to an efficient solar Sweden will increase national security, too. Today's complex, centralized energy system is very easy to turn off, through sabotage, natural disaster, or technical accident. In contrast, a more efficient, diverse, dispersed, renewable energy system could be so resilient that major failures would become impossible. And very high energy productivity, in partnership with renewable sources, could guarantee all Swedes an ample, sustainable, stably priced supply of energy, not just in our own generation, but indefinitely.

A secure and affordable supply of energy, however, is just one of the ingredients of a really secure society. Security also requires other necessities—water, food, shelter. It embraces health, a healthy environment, a flexible and sustainable system of production, a legitimate system of self-government, a durable system of shared values. But where can we get these things which so directly touch our lives and let us all feel safe? Most of all from the institutions nearest to us: from our own efforts, our families, our communities, our local governments. Real security comes less from central governments, dispensed from the top down, than if we build it ourselves from the bottom up. But we cannot feel secure if we enjoy Life, Liberty, and the Pursuit of Happiness while others do not; for then at best we will feel uncomfortable, and we may even fear that others may come to take from us what they lack themselves. Thus we build real security above all when we strive to make our neighbours feel more secure, not less—whether on the scale of the village or the globe.

Real security, too, is not something we can get from armies and missiles. Its roots run deeper and need greater nourishment. It thrives for example, on a political system so firmly based on a common set of values—honed by diverse and vigorous debate—that it cannot be subverted or taken over. On such foundations could even be built, as some Scandinavian strategists have suggested, a standing Resistance that would make one's national territory impossibly disagreeable for anyone else to occupy. Such a purely defensive military posture is cheap; threatens nobody; cannot be perverted into an instrument of oppression; and can even guard against tyranny at home. Such nonmilitary approaches to military problems are an idea whose time is coming fast—and are yet another contribution that Swedish thinking is making to world peace.

From the analysts at SIPRI, to the grassroots activists (such as C. E. Lennart Daleus) who conceived and carried forward the nuclear phase-out referendum, to such courageous advocates of disarmament as Inga Thorsson, many Swedes are contributing to the global ferment of fresh ideas on how to unspread the bomb. Here is a sampling of the wide range of new ideas from around the world on nuclear disarmament:

- Since merely reversing the arms race (i.e. decreasing, instead of increasing, the number of bombs by 4-5%/y) would take 100-200 years to get rid of them, destroy them instead at a rate which increases exponentially. President Reagan, having a flair for the dramatic, could take a Mark 12A warhead to the Nevada Test Site and, on world television, pulverize it with a big sledgehammer—then invite President Andropov (or perhaps a more robust substitute such as Chief of Staff Ogarkov) to do the same with two Soviet warheads, then four American, eight Soviet, etc.

- The past six U.S. Administrations (until this one) have been committed to a Comprehensive Test Ban, but this has always been vetoed by the weapons laboratories. That is because most modern bombs are perishable— they contain tritium and plutonium which decay—so that in time they can no longer be assured of working, unless each vintage has from time to time been taken off the shelf and proof-tested. The U.S. (and perhaps also the Soviet) arsenal is therefore, we are told, to be gradually shifted to all-uranium designs which have an indefinite shelf life and thus need no testing. But we prefer a Comprehensive Test Ban and perishable bombs (on both sides). As the bombs gradually rotted, they would still deter—one could not be sure they would not work—but they would become less and less likely actually to work, so everyone would become safer. A "let 'em rot" policy—coupled, of course, with a comprehensive bilateral freeze so that replacement bombs could not be built—would especially deter a first strike because it would greatly reduce the attacker's confidence of success.

- Our friend and colleague Dr. Donald Westervelt, who for many years ran the bomb-testing program at Los Alamos National Laboratory, points out that it is, and will remain, very difficult to get Superpower agreement about "bean-counting" types of nuclear disarmament (who has how many of what). He therefore proposes building on the existing consensus that short launch times and short warning times are dangerously destabilizing. In nontechnical form, Dr. Westervelt's creative proposal for lengthening launch times would be, for example, to take missiles out of their silos, unbolt the wings from bombers, withdraw all missiles and other nuclear bombs from forward bases (e.g. in Europe), build no means of communicating with submarines much faster than floating them messages in bottles, etc.—and do all of this bilaterally and verifiably. This approach has substantial military support, but no political leader has yet picked up the idea.

- Visits and exchanges by private citizens could be supplemented by a formal revival of the mediaeval concept of mutual hostages: members of the Congress and of the Politburo could send their children to live and study in the other country's main cities.

- The biologist Lewis Thomas proposes that large numbers of U.S. and Soviet troops be given tickets to ride around all the time on each others' railway systems. The revenues would revitalise the railways. Because of the well-known imperfections of railway timetables, nobody would ever know quite where the soldiers were. And as these roving hostages looked out the windows, and discovered that Nebraska and the Ukraine are quite alike, they would recall that there are people out there.

- In a similar vein of rehumanizing the so-called "enemy", there is a new program which arranges for each American family to keep on the mantelpiece of its house the photographs of a Soviet family, and vice versa. There is also a "sister cities" program.

- The Brandt Commission proposed, and Sweden could unilaterally start paying, a rising international tax on arms expenditures. How about a rising megatonnage tax too, to be paid in an annually televised ritual of penance (preferably in Hiroshima or Nagasaki) and distributed to countries without nuclear bombs, as a symbolic (if wholly inadequate) gesture of compensation for the risks imposed on them?

- Better still, every August, each incoming head of state taking office during the previous year, and each head of state of a country having nuclear bombs, should be invited to make a public pilgrimage to the Peace Museum at Hiroshima as guests of the Japanese people. The visitors could see the exhibits, lay wreaths, condemn bombs as a matter for shame rather than pride, and perhaps slip away for a private meeting of Bombaholics Anonymous.

The anthropologist Mary Catherine Bateson offers the

parable of a man who has the habit of drinking himself nightly into oblivion and who, perhaps once a year, gets out his revolver and plays solo Russian roulette. He is killing himself in three ways: the annual gamble with instant death, the slow death of cirrhosis, and the daily rejection of the reality of his being. But these three modes of death feed on each other. When the revolver clicks on an empty cylinder, he thinks he is all right and continues to drink himself to death. He doesn't think too much about what the alcohol is doing to his body because of his overwhelming fear that the Russian roulette will kill him first. The daily oblivion that this fear compels him to seek, keeps him from noticing the creeping cirrhosis or resisting the temptation of the revolver. And so the three go round and round, despair reinforcing itself. In our own world, perhaps once a year, various nuclear alerts are proven false and the nuclear gun doesn't go off. We kill ourselves with the electronic oblivion and "entertainment" to which our fears drive us. These too feed on each other, and the steady revolving of the insane merry-go-round can be jammed only by minute particulars of work and hope. But first, like the alcoholic, we must face the depth of our addictive predicament. Breaking the numbed silence of dread will require new rituals, new symbolisms, and above all new actions by millions of ordinary people.

This is not to deny the deep divisions in the world—least of all those between Soviet and American leaders, who seem to deny their common humanity, and to share only a preference for their own people alive to the other's people dead. But these hostile, suspicious, fearful leaders will have to live together whether or not they trust each other. If, after all, they could trust each other, there would be no need for arms control, because there would be no "need" for arms. And our leaders, like all of us, had better start getting used to the idea that nuclear bombs are not the problem; they are only a symptom. The problem is war: and, underlying war, the legacy of tribalism, human aggression, injustice, power without purpose, the psychic premises of eons of homo-centric, patriarchal, imperial culture. If we as a species do not squarely address these problems, nuclear disarmament will only buy time before we find some other ingenious way of killing each other.

The transformation of human values that can alone provide lasting security can only come from within each of us. It begins with you and me as we talk to each other and then to others. That is exactly how, for example, the Zen poet Gary Snyder stopped the war in Vietnam. In the mid 1960s, Gary was sitting in a bar in Tokyo and fell into conversation with a fellow American who was on his way to Saigon to do a government study of the war. The stranger was so surprised and fascinated to find that Gary thought the war a bad idea that he postponed his trip to Saigon and they talked for three days about the war, about values and philosophy. When they parted, Gary didn't think much would come of it. But some years later, having moved back to California and lived in several places, Gary got word on the grapevine that someone on a motorcycle had been looking for him, chasing him from one old address to the next. The searcher had finally sent forward a message to Gary, saying: "I'm the guy you met in that bar in Tokyo. That conversation changed my life. Watch your newspaper." A few weeks later, the Pentagon Papers story broke. The guy was Dan Ellsberg.

It matters whom you talk to. It matters that you care. Peace will break out when enough of us have peace in our hearts. Peace will blossom when enough of us ask ourselves each night, "What have I done today to help my neighbour feel more secure?"—and when we like the answer. We shall have peace-when we each take personal responsibility for it.

Within your genes and mine is the legacy of thousands of millions of years of biological wisdom, evolving unbroken to this day. Within your genes and mine is the heritage of all children yet unborn, their potential for all time entrusted to our stewardship. Let us, in their name, choose life.

THE GREEN MOVEMENT
Petra Kelly
9th December, 1982

*"Oh sisters, come you sing for all you're worth. Arms are
made for linking, sisters, we are asking for the Earth"*

EMMA GOLDMAN wrote: "True emancipation begins
neither at the polls nor in the courts, it begins in women's
soul. History tells us that every oppressed class gained true
liberation from its masters through its own efforts. It is
necessary that women learn from that lesson, that they
realize that their freedom will reach as far as their power to
achieve their freedom reaches."

The true essence of Emma Goldman's feminist vision
was that women should start taking responsibility for their
own lives, insted of trying to improve or purify the lives of
men. Emma Goldman explained that male egotism, vanity
and strength in the patriarchal sense, operated to enslave
women. It was partly, she argued, because women themselves
often idolized those qualities in men, creating a self-
perpetuating system.

Women must change their consciousness, break from
the patriarchal circle and free themselves from such ill-suited
ideals as those of the masculine, patriarchal and nuclear
society. For too long we have been told that to gain equal
chances and equal opportunities, we must accept the equal
rights and equal duties of men. But it cannot be

emancipation, to stand beside men in the various national armies and learn to shoot and learn to kill. It cannot be emancipation to learn to operate a nuclear reactor or to be able to sit in a nuclear silo and operate the control board.

The development of women, their freedom, their independence, must come from, and through, themselves. Firstly by asserting themselves as human beings and not as sex commodities. Secondly by refusing the right to anyone over their bodies, by refusing to bear children unless they want them. By refusing to be a servant to the state, society, husband, family—by making their lives deeper and richer. That is, by trying to learn the meaning and substance of life in all its complexities, by freeing themselves from the fear of public opinion and public condemnation. These words again are drawn from Emma Goldman, who tried to help women to free themselves from bondage to state and husband.

I begin with this vision of the strong women in history, because without the emancipation of women, and without the emancipation of men, we cannot build a non-violent, ecological and non-military green republic. The women of the "Pentagon action" of November 1980 explained why they were holding hands, and why they were engaging in direct non-violent action: "We are in the hands of men whose power and wealth have separated them from the reality of daily life and from the imagination. We are right to be afraid."

There is fear among the people, and that fear, created by the industrial militarists, is used as an excuse to accelerate the arms race. "We will protect you . . .", they say, but we have never been so endangered, so close to the end of human time. Women are gathering because life on the precipice is intolerable. We want to know what anger in these men, what fear which can only be satisfied by destruction, what coldness of heart and ambition, drives their days? We want to know, because we do not want that dominance, which is exploitative and murderous in international relations, and so dangerous to women and children at home—we do not want that sickness transferred by a violent society, through fathers to sons.

While women and men will be blockading many nuclear installations on the 12th of December 1982, whether in Bitburg/Germany, or Greenham Common/Great Britain, or Stockholm/Sweden, the vertical and horizontal arms race is continuing. The vertical arms race, in which the main contestants are the USA and USSR, is the continuous attempt to gain numerical and technological superiority. Already, this vertical arms race has led to the mad state of affairs known as overkill, in which the stock piles of nuclear weapons are now considerably more than enough to destroy every human being on the earth 40 times over.

The world is also involved in a horizontal arms race, in which more and more nations acquire the potential to produce nuclear weapons. During this decade, many countries will be able to come within hours of the production of the bomb, (including many nations which have agreed to abstain from making one) without actually violating the non-proliferation agreement. The bomb and the reactor cannot, in the eyes of the European peace, ecological, and women's movements, be separated. They are truly Siamese twins, swords from so-called plough-shares. The military potential of the civilian use of nuclear energy has been underestimated, not only by the Christian-Democratic governments who are continuing to build more nuclear plants, reactors and reprocessing facilities.

The military potential of nuclear energy has also been underestimated by the Social-Democratic or Socialist Governments, whether in the Federal Republic of Germany, or in Great Britain or Sweden. We, the forces of the international anti-war and anti-nuclear weapons movement, must be honest and must reject all nuclear power plants, all nuclear facilities, whether civilian or military. The Israeli attack on the nuclear reactor in Iraq; increasing sales of nuclear reactors to Brazil, Argentina and Pakistan; the fact that a country with an extensive civilian nuclear power programme cannot be defended by military means; and the fact that low level radiation from man-made sources is causing a cancerous, dying world population, must mobilize us to reject the process of nuclearization everywhere.

By 1985, about 40 countries will have enough missile material to make three bombs or more. Almost as many are likely to have enough missile material for 30 to 60 of such weapons or more. Existing civilian nuclear activities have, as a by-product, advanced many countries a long way towards the production of atomic weapons-grade material. Furthermore, since civilian nuclear activities overlap with military ones, they can provide a cover-up for further military advance.

More than 50,000 nuclear bombs, over 1 million Hiroshimas worth, already hang over the world, and their number grows daily. At this present time Ronald Reagan and the United States government subsidize more reactors for South Korea, and pressure the Philippines to continue their work on reactors. The USSR speeds up its reactor programme and exports nuclear supplies to the Third World. France develops neutron bombs. The United Kingdom announces programmes to make its own tritium and highly enriched uranium. Germany is about to build commercial reprocessing plants and has just given the green light to the Fast Breeder in Kalkar. This world continues to spend over half a trillion Dollars a year—a million Dollars per minute—on more efficient ways to kill people! And this is in 1982, some days before Christmas! In an era where the total explosive power released in World War II is encapsulated in single bombs that can fit beneath a bed, the conviction grows: WE SHALL ALL BLOW EACH OTHER UP; THE ONLY QUESTION IS WHEN (Amory Lovins). Beyond the fear and denial of this syndrome of "terminality" (bureaucratization of homicide) is the enjoyment of the simple things left to us. It is a song, a walk in a meadow, seeing a child smile—must we accept the absence of a future? Have we a future?

"Wars will cease when men refuse to fight". This statement has attracted many to the pacifist philosophy which is an integral part of the Green Party, the alternative party and non-violent movement which I have helped to build up since leaving the Social Democratic Party in 1978. The Green Party within the Fedral Republic of Germany is at the moment the only hope I have to change not only the system of structural and personal violence, but also to find a way out of the insane policies of atomic deterrence. The Green Party, to which I have dedicated my efforts and all my energy in the past three years, is committed to basic democracy, to ecology in the broadest sense of the term, to social justice and to non-violence. Military leaders and politicians have in the past aroused partial unity by means of fear, pride, anger, hate and lies. Unity can also be aroused by love and the desire for social justice. When a sufficient number of people begin to understand the close relationships between the arms race and international violence, economic deprivation, social injustice, and ecological instability, then we are on the way to make the right demands for the benefit of humankind, rather than for one nation, one particular class. The global overview of military and social expenditures as presented by the Stockholm Institute for Peace Reasearch (SIPRI) make grim reading. It is a dismal reflection of our values as a world community. We have thought it necessary to invest so much more of our wealth in military power than in meeting the needs of society, in meeting the needs of women, children and men.

The Green Party has an underlying value which states clearly that humankind must not consider the land and what it supports in terms of private property and real estate. We are all temporary custodians of the land—entrusted to us for passing on unimpared to future generations. We argue that the most urgent and most straight forward disarmament measures required from an ecological standpoint are the absolute prohibition of all nuclear weapons, of all atomic, biological, chemical weapons and a complete demilitarization and conversion to protective status of ecologically important regions. Nuclear power states now comprise a large part of the world's population. There is for me only one way out— complete unilateral disarmament. The bilateral, step by step, approaches have failed. We propose unilateral and calculated steps towards complete disarmament as a solution not only for the Federal Republic of Germany, but for all European countries, for all countries in the world. Each government must take that first step which it expects other governments to take! If governments do not take these first steps, we shall take them! We must work towards a disarmament race. Military balances, the balance of terror, the counting-game, are irrelevant. The greatest criticism that can be made of the nuclear arms race is its total irrelevance to the problems facing us today. World poverty, diminishing natural resources, overpopulation, and pollution—these are the problems we face today. The only war we seek should be the war against humankind's ancient enemies—povery, hunger, illiteracy and preventable disease.

The anti-war and anti-nuclear movement does not mean negative protest. It is necessarily pro-environment, pro-woods and pro-fields, pro-rivers and oceans, pro-plants and animals, pro-solar energy, pro-clean air and above all, pro-people. It is a planetary vision, a planetary moral standard, for hungry people, poor people, women, youth, the handicapped, the old people, the Amazon tribes, the Aborigines, the inner-city slum dwellers, the oppressed minorities everywhere—we are all in this together. We are in fact the realists, we are not only the dreamers of brother and sisterhood, of non-violence and of survival.

When I think of the non-violence we need, not only in the course of politics, but as a way of life, I think of the native Americans, the American Indians, who have a reverence for life, who respect human dignity and understand the inter-connection of all things to an extent that has yet to be surpassed. The genocide perpetrated by the United States on the Indian tribes and cultures—a pattern which still continues today—remains one of the most crucial indict-ments of white civilization. In 1854, Chief Seattle, leader of the Suquamish-tribe in the Washington territory, delivered this prophetic speech to mark the transferral of ancestral Indian lands to the Federal Government: ". . . this we know. The Earth does not belong to man; man belongs to the Earth, this we know. All things are connected like the blood which unites one family. All things are connected. Whatever befalls the Earth, befalls the sons of the Earth. Man did not weave the web of life, he is merely a part of it. Whatever he does to the web, he does to himself."

This is perhaps another way of saying that we must build up the power of the people, which will be a power different from the power of the state. We need to restructure and overhaul the entire social fabric, for it is at this moment woven by violence. I want both peace and a non-violent revolution. If we want peace, then as Mahatma Gandhi has said, the only way to peace is peace itself. We have to prove that non-violence and peace have the power to revolutionize society. Non-violence is a relatively new idea which differs considerable from religious pacifism. While pacifism refers to the traditional belief that all killing, particularly in war, is wrong, contemporary non-violence concerns itself with the implications of this belief in the whole social fabric. Non-violence implies a broader definition of what causes and constitutes violence. It takes the initiative against the existing system of dominance and privilege, and gives more conscious attention to the building of an alternative social structure. War and the war system, the military industrial complex in the West and bureaucratic repression in the East, as well as social violence, are inherent in our present political-economic order and prevailing materialistic culture. A.J. Muste wrote that humanity faced a major crisis in which only drastic change, such as is suggested by the terms rebirth and conversion, can bring deliverance. Muste called for a non-violent revolutionary movement which would include both changes in external relationships and an inner transformation of the individual. That is to say that while we are fighting against the larger war, the ABC-war, we must, at the same time, also fight against the small wars; the wars of violence that take place every day in our streets where women fear to walk alone at night; that take place every time a woman is raped or beaten, every time a child is hit. We need not only to change the status quo of institutionalized violence, but also to change ourselves fundamentally before we can change social and political life.

Non-violence in the tradition of Martin Luther King, of Gandhi and Bertha von Suttner, is a natural element which relies on the power of truth rather than the force of arms, and which flows from a sense of the underlying unity of all human beings. At the same time there can be no sustained non-violent struggles unless social institutions based on non-violent principles are built up. Non-violent resistance and direct action are an extremely important part of this movement, on a European and worldwide basis. Yet at the root of non-violence is unity based on love, and the desire for justice and constructive work, which will build up the structure of the new global society. Conscience must become stronger than custom, and personal risks must be taken to better the common lot. I think at this stage especially about the brave initiatives of the Catholic bishops in the United States, on the questions of nuclear disarmament. I think of Bishop Raymond Hunthausen who has been initiating a tax-strike since April of 1982 with the consequence of perhaps having to go to jail. I think of Daniel Ellsberg and the many men and women who sat on the railroad tracks in Rocky Flats to stop a plutonium train. I think of the farmers in Comiso/Italy who are trying to help buy the property to prevent the siting of Cruise Missiles which will point at Libya. I think of the "other America", which is now engaged in the Freeze Campaign, and I think of the many Japanese sisters and brothers who, together with our friends in the Pacific, are marching for a nuclear-free world. And I think of our sisters and brothers in Eastern Europe, whether in Solidarnosc or within the East German peace movement, working under the symbol of "Swords into plough-shares".

The vision I see is not only a movement of direct democracy, of self- and co-determination and of non-violence, but a movement in which politics means the power to love and the power to feel united on spaceship Earth. We need life affirming directions in politics, and thus the Green Party will never compromise on the issues of life and death, on the issues of the right to life, the right to health, to peace, the right to a safe and healthy environment. Such issues cannot be compromised and cannot be misused for the sake of staying in power or gaining power. In the Federal Elections the Greens will not, in any of those question of life and death, make one compromise, for if we did make such a compromise we would betray not only our voters but also our members and the movement. In a world struggling in violence and dishonesty, the further development of non-violence not only as a philosophy but as an effective political force on the streets, in the market squares, outside the missile bases, inside the chemical plants and inside the war industry, becomes one of the most urgent priorities.

The vision I have is the vision of social or civilian defence, a world in which we not only abolish destructive weapons, but also the so-called military security and defence system. If we believe strongly enough in our democratic ideas, if we believe in our rights of speech and rights of assembly, in our rights of conscience, then no tank and no missile can blackmail or repress us. Social defence, which is a highly sophisticated form of non-violent direct action (should there be a so-called aggressor from within or at one's borders), makes the price for the aggressor so high that he will have to think twice before ever attempting an invasion. Social defence calls for a democratized society, and calls for society built up on mutual solidarity.

Not only the Reagan administration, but all administrations which call for increased military spending, are committing an act of aggression which amounts to a crime, for even when they are not used, by their cost alone armaments kill the poor by causing misery and deprivation. In any attempt to measure the arms race this is the bottom line: death by deprivation is surely as heinous as death by force of arms.

Our young people don't need the draft, they need jobs: our older people don't need new weapons of overkill, they need better housing at more affordable prices. Our working people cannot live with the inflationary effects of military spending, they need the right to a job, they need the right to work, and the right to good work. People who are ill don't need Cruise missiles, they need affordable health care. We do not need the SS 20 or the MX missile, but an efficient mass transit system. We must bring together on this planet Earth the different groups which have worked in isolation. We must form a grass roots alliance based on shared interests if we are to reach out effectively to a larger audience. We need to develop a non-violent strategy, not only to stop the deployment of first strike missiles in Europe, but to begin the removal of all weapons of mass destruction and finally to get rid of them. And I make a last appeal not only to the Peace Movement in Europe, but to the Third World movement everywhere. Women and children of the Third World are to perish first. They have already begun to starve. All that is asked of them is to starve quietly. The tragedy of women in the Third World is one that moves me, touches me deeply. There are now about a hundred million children under the age of five always hungry. Fifteen million children die every year from infection and malnutrition, and there are about 800 million illiterates in the world, nearly two thirds of them women. While I say this I remember at the same time the multi-national company Nestle that has told women in the Third World to stop breast-feeding and to start feeding lactogen. All this is related directly to our own prosperity, and to so-called material and economic growth. The developed nations are armed to the teeth, and mean not only to hold on to what they have, but to grasp everything they can. The suffering people of this world must come together to take control of their lives, to wrest political power from their present masters who are pushing them towards destruction. The Earth has been mistreated—only by restoring a balance, only by living with the Earth, only by employing knowledge and expertise towards soft energies and soft technology, a technology for people and for life, can we overcome the patriarchal ego.

The police and atomic state, and the danger of totalitarian regimes, created in the name of making secure the nuclear societies, are not far away. We must lose our fears; we must speak up, and we must demand what is ours and what is our children's. We must begin to rediscover our own nature, we must begin to forge new ways , ways of wholeness, inter-connectedness, balance, preservation and decentralisation. As Gandhi said, the non-violence of the weak must become the non-violence of the brave. I believe that unarmed truth and unconditional love will have the final word in reality.

THE GREEN BELT MOVEMENT IN KENYA

Wangari Maathai

9th December 1984

THE GREEN BELT Movement (GBM) is now a slogan which describes a broad-based grass-root tree planting activity currently taking place in Kenya. Since trees are planted in several rows around compounds or farm plots (shambas), the planting of trees appears to dress up the compounds in belts of green trees. In our adverse activities on the land (e.g. indiscriminate cutting down of trees, bush clearing, failure to stop soil erosion, overgrazing, over-population and overall general negligence towards our environment), not only have we torn into rags the beautiful green dress of our mother-land but in some places we have stripped her naked. We have inflicted deep wounds on her and she is weak and unproductive. Yes, indeed, according to the prophet Isaiah, we have sinned against the Natural Laws (God, goodness, order of Nature) and we are being punished. The Natural Laws are taking their natural course which for us means destruction and death. We must repent our sins (i.e. rectify our wrong doings) by dressing our mother, our mother-land, in her original beautiful and full green dress. In planting trees we are adorning our mother-land with belts.

When we have repented (i.e. rectified) our mother-land will be healed and we shall reap a bounteous harvest. And thus our committal, which we recite before planting trees:

"Being aware that Kenya is being threatened by the expansion of desert-like conditions, that desertification comes as a result of misuse of the land by indiscriminate cutting-down of trees, bush clearing and consequent soil erosion by the elements; and that these actions result in drought, malnutrition, famine and death, WE RESOLVE to save our land by averting this same desertification by tree planting wherever possible".

"In pronouncing these words, we each make a personal commitment to our country to save it from actions and elements which would deprive present and future generations from reaping the bounty which is the birthright and property of all".

Why we do what we do.

The Kenya Government has a Ministry of Environment and Natural Resources and a Presidential Commission on Soil Conservation and re-afforestation. Both bodies are responsible for re-afforestation efforts in the whole country. But we know that few governments, and less so in the developing world, can afford the financial and man-power resources required to do what needs to be done.

It is necessary for private/voluntary, non-governmental organizations (NGOs) and individuals to be mobilized to provide at least the man-power needed in afforestation programmes.

As soon as we took trees to the people we realized that there was great demand for them. People clamoured for the trees we issued at public meetings. This was a pleasant sight. Unfortunately, we also discovered that they did not appreciate the fact that trees, like other crops, need to be planted properly, need after-care and have to be sheltered from livestock and human beings. It became obvious to us that there was need to teach almost all the people that they have to dig holes, apply manure, make sure that water is available and build a shelter for protection.

The demand for trees necessitated the establishment of tree nurseries. In order to take more trees to a greater number of people we realized the need to train ordinary people to become seedling producers. Since we are a Women's organisation, and many women are organized into groups, we decided to make rural women our major target group. We trained them on the basics of raising seedlings more or less in the same way that they can raise their cabbages and potatoes. These groups have now been joined by youth groups and clubs.

In order to promote seedling production, we decided to purchase them at a minimal price of about US seven cents per seedling. This way, not only do the groups gain new and useful knowledge but tree production becomes income-generating.

Most people are crop-farmers and livestock-keepers. They cannot turn all their land into woodlots because they need it for crops. They are encouraged to practise agroforestry, farming methods our people used before the European methods of farming were introduced and erroneously considered superior. Now the scientists are recommending this agroforestry approach and unfortunately the current generation has to be taught to inter-crop all over again. This requires some knowledge of the trees, and the role they play in the soil and in respect to other crops. Most indigenous trees, for example, are of course better suited ecologically but many are slow growing and do not have much economic value in the current market. This puts them at a disadvantage as farmers go for the exotic or imported trees which grow faster and have a well established market— that is, at least to-day, when the trees grow in what is to them virgin land. Several hundred years from now we may find that the exotic trees precipitated desertification and destruction of the varied life that exists in tropical ecological systems. To discourage the planting of imported trees, we pay less to seedling producers (mostly women) for them and more for the indigenous and fruit trees which are more appropriate for agroforestry.

The original major objective of the green belt movement was to help the needy urban poor of a certain area of Nairobi. In mind were the handicapped, school leavers and the very poor. The best way to help them was to create jobs. So we hired them as green belt rangers and nursery attendants.

Many of the green belt rangers and nursery attendants are illiterate, and have no training in nursery or forestry techniques. We would provide them with basic training to enable them to nurse the trees and assist the school children, each of whom attends a few trees. By employing such persons we were also, indirectly, rehabilitating and assisting them amongst their relatives and friends instead of having them institutionalized, moved to towns where they become beggars.

Whenever possible we try to employ mothers or fathers so that the whole family benefits. We have had situations where the handicapped person is assisted by his/her able-bodied companion.

The nursery attendants supervise the operations at the nursery. They help keep records, make monthly reports, and issue the trees to the members of the public. They also teach newcomers to the nursery the basics of how to produce seedlings for sale to the green belt movement.

We noted that when the community identifies a person who could play this role, they would mostly identify a very poor parent whose children may be having problems with school fees.

Besides the very poor and the handicapped, school leavers are hired as promoters and follow-ups.

The promoters go ahead of everybody else in the field and talk to the members of the community about the problems of desertification, giving suggestions on what they can individually do, encouraging them to dig holes and apply manure to them. They send monthly reports on the number of holes they check, and issue approval tokens which the applicants take to the nurseries so that they can be issued with trees. The green belt movement expands as fast and well as the promoters can effectively push it to the members of the public.

The follow-ups attend to the planted trees to ensure that they are indeed planted, that they are being attended to and that they are therefore surviving. They also send in monthly reports on the number of trees issued and the number surviving at the green belts.

A few trained individuals are engaged as supervisors in the field. When operating at peak there may be 250-300 individuals earning their living from this programme. If we were able to create substantially more jobs in the rural areas we would help in curbing migration into the urban areas in search of jobs. Most migrants are the young and the rural poor. Migration into the urban centres only served to aggravate the unemployment situation, and the problem of the urban poor who live in shanties and city peripheral areas.

One of the most obvious results of deforestation and bush clearing is soil erosion. During the rainy seasons rivers are red with the top soil. Lost top soil leaves behind impoverished sub-soil which cannot support agriculture, and as a result food production goes down. Education is necessary so that farmers can appreciate the relationship between soil erosion and poor agricultural output.

Deforestation and bush clearing have precipitated an energy crisis because woodfuel has become scarce. Fetching of wood and preparation of food for the family is a responsibility of the women. And so as wood disappears women and children walk further and further from home to look for firewood, which may only turn out to be twigs and sticks. Where these do not exist they will turn to agricultural residues and cowdung. These are products which should be returned to the soil in order to make it richer for food production. Burning these breaks the carbon-cycle and creates a vicious circle in agricultural production.

The crisis of woodfuel precipitates another problem: malnutrition. A woman with little woodfuel opts to give her family food that requires little energy to prepare. If she has money, she often turns to refined foods like bread, maize meal, tea and soft drinks. A woman may not appreciate what she must give her family to ensure a balanced diet. That ignorance, coupled with shortage of woodfuel, provides the background for undernourishment and disease associated with poor feeding habits. If too many people are caught up in this situation one can easily have a sick society, and a sick society is unproductive. Unproductive people are eventually pushed down into the world of underdevelopment. It is very important, therefore, that the energy crisis of the poor is solved through provision of the wood and the utilization of more efficient combustion devices which reduce wood consumption.

Indirectly, the project has been promoting a positive image of women, a concern for the National Council of Women in Kenya (NCWK) which strives to promote a balanced development of a woman's personality and to facilitate an environment in which such development can take place. Even after ten years of debate on womens' issues during the women decade, it appears appropriate for women to talk around development issues and cause positive change in themselves and their country. Development issues provide a good forum for women to be creative, assertive and effective leaders and the green belt movement, being a development issue, provided the forum to promote a positive image of women.

This is very important, because women have to become involved in development as equal participants and benefactors. Currently, although women are the most numerous voters, very few are voted into public office. This is partially because women are not afforded a forum to develop leadership qualities as they mature, and even during adulthood. They are always the followers but never the leaders. Women are, therefore, too often only nominated by men to positions of responsibility. Women have always played a major role in the socio-economic and political arena of nations but they are not always publicly acclaimed, appreciated or proportionately rewarded. Indeed, they are often silenced by small token positions of influence and responsibility while men are rewarded with positions they hardly deserve. Women have generally come to accept that they have to be extremely grateful for the very little they get from men, both in private and public fora. Those women who would point out the continued disproportionate representation of women in the decision-making structure (both political and economic) are conveniently given such labels as rebels, radicals, womens libbers, elites, and so forth. This is deliberately done to discredit them in the eyes of the public, so that whatever they have to say or stand for is suspiciously scrutinized and preferably scorned.

Because of this, the majority of women will opt for practices which dehumanize them and make them weak, unchallenging servants to their menfolk rather than partners in development. As in other areas of inequality deliberately promoted, the myths of the inferiority of women can only be demolished though glaring examples with which nobody can intelligently argue. The green belt movement and other projects initiated by women are some examples around which kitchens, babies, nappies and sex are not the points of reference:

Most of the short term objectives have been realised. Some of these are:

(a) To encourage tree planting so as to provide the source of energy in the rural areas.

(b) To promote planting of multipurpose trees with special reference to the nutritional and energy requirements of man and his livestock.

(c)   To promote the protection and maintainance of the environment and development through seminars, conferences, workshops, etc.

(d)   To encourage soil conservation, land reclamation and rehabilitation through tree planting.

(e)   To develop methods for rational land use.

(f)   To create an income-generating activity for rural women.

(g)   To create self-employment opportunities especially for handicapped persons and the rural poor.

(h)   To develop a replicable methodology for rural development.

(i)   To carry out research in conjunction with the University of Nairobi and other research institutions.

(j)   To create self-employment opportunities for young persons.

(k)   To carry out any activities that promote these objectives.

Thousands of trees have been produced by women, and planted by communities and school children in over 700 public green belts. Thousands of individuals have established private green belts. Tree planting has become an honourable activity for all, and because the political leadership publicly supports conservation and reafforestation efforts, the general populace is easily persuaded. The sight of the President planting a tree and urging others to do the same is a valuable example for his people to emulate.

Community tree nurseries operated by womens' groups, youth clubs and schools have been established in many parts of the country. At the moment there are about fifty. Not only are the trees generating income for the producers, but relevant knowledge is being imparted to them during demonstration sessions and visits by the trained personnel.

Scores of individuals, especially the poor and the

handicapped, have found jobs within their own environment amongst friends and relatives. Some children have completed their schooling because their parents were employed as green belt rangers.

Why has this approach worked?

Many people have wanted to know why the approach we have opted for has worked. There are a combination of reasons. Some of the more obvious are as follows:

- The green belt movement pursues several goals at the same time and focusses on several target groups, all of whom can find their place in the movement.
- The short-term objectives are realized fast enough to maintain momentum and interest. People need success stories to emulate.
- The Executive Committee of NCWK, and those directly charged with the responsibility of guiding the movement, have been very committed.
- There has been a good understanding of the issues involved. The leaders appreciated the cost of the high rate of population growth against the scarce land resource; they knew of the diminishing forest cover; they appreciated that the elimination of indigenous trees would precipitate a changed ecosystem. They felt that because they knew, it was their responsibility to initiate action.

Who has funded the movement?

Initially, we worked with purely voluntary service, which in our country is know as harambee. Then we introduced the idea of sponsoring trees which we would plant and take care of. Some substantial donations came from Mobil Oil (UK) Ltd.; the Environment Liaison Center; the Canadian Embassy; the German Embassy; and the International Council of Women. The total amounted to Kshs. 160,000 (about US Dollars 10,000). In 1981 we hit a jackpot and received Kshs. 1 million (US Dollars 100,000) from the Voluntary Fund of the United Nations; Kshs. ½ million (US Dollars 50,000) from the Norwegian Forestry Society and Norad; and Kshs. 3½ million (US Dollars 350,000) from the Danish Voluntary Fund for Developing Countries. All the grants have run currently and are scheduled to end before or in 1985. We have just received financial support from Norad of Kshs. 1.9 million (US Dollars 127,000).

What we do with the funds.

We purchase tools for tree nurseries and green belts, organize workshops and seminars for new participants, purchase seedlings from seedling producers (mostly women), pay green belt staff (nursery attendants, promoters, follow-ups, green belt rangers and supervisors), and maintain a small secretariat at the headquarters. The ordinary people contribute in kind by:-

> Digging holes for tree planting;
> Providing manure;
> Sheltering, protecting and watering the trees;
> Preparing nursery sites, including making benches, seedbeds, etc.
> Collecting seeds.

Many of our members supervise the operations in the fields and assist with on site training for new participants.

I am often asked, "Why did it take the women to start the green belt movement?"

The inspiration did not come to me because I was a woman. It came to me because my mind was searching for a solution to a very specific problem. Inspirations come to all of us but many of us may not have the right mental peace and tranquility at the critical time to allow the inspiration to grow beyond the stage when it appears like a dream. I think I was just lucky. I do not know why I nursed the inspiration until it became an idea and finally an activity. I think that women in the NCWK were quite good at pursuing an idea which for a long time bore little fruit. But patience is not a prerogative of women. Men could have done the same if inspired and sufficiently motivated. Perhaps the only thing that was characteristically women-like was our grouping and our rapid acceptance of the movement. But some observers claim that this motivating force in the field, especially among women, was the financial gain. May be, may be not. But if it is, very few men were so motivated until much, much later.

Liaison has been essential because of the nature of the project. The green belt movement has worked closely with the Ministry of Environment & Natural Resources from the very beginning. At a very early stage, it was possible for our participants to walk into the forester's office and receive as many seedlings as had been prepared. Most, if not all, foresters have co-operated in this endeavour and all appreciate the complimentary and rather unique contribution being made by the green belt movement.

There has also been very close co-operation with the office of the President (Administration) which has assisted at the district and local levels. The green belt staff are often invited to meetings to explain the movement to the people.

Each green belt or tree nursery is supervised by a local committee, comprised of leaders from the local community. This is the committee which maintains the spirit of interest and awareness after the NCWK's launching party has gone. It is the nucleus around which the community will continue to be motivated and involved. Under the leadership of the local green belt committee, community volunteers dig holes, place manure in them and wait for the launching ceremony. Under the current method such work, which would otherwise cost the tax payer a lot of money and time, is given free-of-charge by the community.

What of the future?

We must continue to care about issues which are not immediately concerned with the gratification of our physical senses. We are a unique heritage to the ecosystem on this planet earth and we have a special responsibility. If to those to whom more has been given, more will be expected, then we must embrace our special responsibility, which is more than is expected of the elephants and the butterflies. In making sure that they and their future generations survive we shall be ensuring the survival of our own species. Where people have been insensitive to the life of trees, to the life that flourishes in the top soil of cropland, of grass and shrubs, of young children, . . . yes, of all living things—we have witnessed indiscriminate deforestation, soil erosion, over-grazing, over-population, drought, desertification, famine and death.

More that sixty per cent of Kenya's land is no longer available to the farmer; forests stand at the low level of 2.5%, some river levels have fallen to a minimum before they disappear altogether. Crop yields have fallen, livestock industry is not what it used to be, and our towns have many who are poor and unemployed. But we continue to cross bridges in our beautiful cars and aeroplanes, and only give a passing glance to the muddy waters below. We cut our age-old indigenous trees to replace them with fast growing and economically valuable exotic ever-greens, and we refuse to exert pressure where we should to avoid being unpopular. Yet Kenya is not among the worst in Africa. We must then go beyond Kenya and help raise public awareness in other parts of the Continent.

The financial reward will be used to establish a Trust which could be used to provide seed money for the establishment of programmes similar to the green belt movement elsewhere in Africa. We are confident that once we start, such an effort would appeal to others who are concerned about desertification processes, prolonged drought, famine and death in our region. I thank you therefore, on my own behalf, on behalf of all the beneficiaries both current and those in years to come. I thank you for caring, for appreciating and for rewarding. I am encouraged, strengthened and inspired by your kindness and generosity of heart and mind.

THE ENVIRONMENT
IN EASTERN EUROPE

Janos Vargha (on behalf of Duna Kor)

9th December 1985

I WOULD like to cite a story, more than two hundred years old, which happened to Gulliver's host in Lagado: "He had a very convenient mill turned by a current from a large river, and sufficient for his own family as well as a great number of his tenants. Then about seven years ago a club of projectors came to him with proposals to destroy his mill, and build another on the side of the mountain, on the long ridge whereof a long canal must be cut for a repository of water, to be conveyed up by pipes and engines to supply the mill . . . The water descending down a declivity would turn the mill with half the current of a river whose course is more upon a level. He said that being then not very well with the court, and pressed by many of his friends, he complied with the proposal; and after employing an hundred men for two years, the work miscarried, the projectors went off, laying the blame entirely upon him, railing at him ever since, and putting others upon the same experiment, with equal assurance of success, as well as equal disappointment."

Since that time zealous projectors have been diligently transforming nature; their marks can be found on the rivers Volga, on the Nile and the Tennessee, as well as on the Waitaki River in New Zealand. There are several serious consequences. For example, the Caspian Sea in the USSR is shrinking irresistibly; schistosomiais has spread in Egypt; the fish population at the mouth of the Nile has decreased; and the land alongside the Rhine in Baden province has dried out.

The work of the projectors and their high protectors is going to be more and more difficult: they encounter people living alongside the rivers, who strongly defend the values of their homelands.

Still, their defence remains usually unsuccessful. Brazil has wasted billions of dollars on the Itaipu Dam, the reservoir of which will be silted up within a short time. The Victoria Dam in Sri Lanka is under construction with British financial "help", destroying 7000 acres of fertile land for only 210 megawatts. Bavaria intends to complete the construction of the Rhine-Main-Danube Canal at any price.

On the other hand the Chico Dam project in the Philippines was suspended after massive local resistance. In the USSR, Zaligin, a Russian writer and engineer, has successfully prevented the construction of a useless and harmful barrage of the lower section of the River Ob. Moreover, Austrian environmentalists recently defended the Danubian forests at Hainburg with their own bodies.

In order to protect the Danubian environment our group, the Duna Kor, participates in the opposition to a large hydroelectric power plant system at Gabcikovo-Nagymaros. This project consists of a $60km^2$ storage lake; a 30km long concrete covered lateral canal rising 18 meters over the ground at a peak power station of Gabcikovo; and an additional river power plant at Nagymaros, in the lovely Danube-bend.

The project would essentially change the hydraulic, physical, chemical and biological conditions of a nearly two hundred kilometer long section of the river itself, as well as that of the surrounding groundwater. These changes would be harmful to the drinking water supply, the quality of river and ground water, agriculture, forests, and fish—as well as the picturesque landscape. The project was planned some decades ago to produce maximum energy and to excessively increase waterway capacity, (not required by the heaviest traffic imaginable, on this section of the river). In addition, this would be relatively the most expensive electric power plant built in Hungary. Twice as much energy could be saved at the same price if money were spent on rationalizing energy consumption. The project has become a perfect nonsense, taking its harmful ecological consequences into consideration. The question of drinking water supply has enormous importance because of its generally serious situation in Hungary and also in Slovakia.

Of Hungary's 3,500 settlements, 1,500 have no potable water. Two and a half million people living in these regions get their drinking water supply in plastic bags or tank cars, or, short of these, have to make do with contaminated water.

By the diversion of 97.5 per cent of the mean flow rate of the river to the sealed side canal, Czechoslovakia and Hungary will lose essential bank filtered water resources of an estimated 2.5 million m^3/day capacity, all of excellent quality. A significant part of this resource is officially registered in Hungary as a long-range reserve, enough to supply three million people at least. The estimated 13 km^3 potable water stored in the deep alluvial sediment would be gradually polluted, as the diversion of the river terminates the continuous supply of this great underground reservoir by large amounts of filtered Danube waters (which dilutes and removes polluting materials originating from agriculture, industry and households). In the reach of the other barrage of Nagymaros, the bank filtered water resources would be endangered by the silting up of the river bed. Austrian and Yugoslav experience of Danubian barrages suggests the deterioration of water quality, as well as a significant decrease in water producing capacity.

Unfortunately, these and other aspects have been completely omitted from the decision taken to build this hydroelectric power plant system. One explanation for this may be historical. The political and technical archetype of the Gabcikovo-Nagymaros project is the so-called Grand Alsatian Canal, on the border section of the Rhine between France and Germany. Due to environmental damage, France gave up her exceptional rights to this canal, included in the Versailles Peace Treaty. The construction of the canal was stopped in the 1950's, half way between Basel and Strasbourg.

We regard the Gabcikovo-Nagymaros project to be a hisorical mistake, from political and social points of view as well as from the aspect of the ecological importance of the Danube. We also regard Austrian participation, whereby they would receive energy, (at the cost of harming the environment of neighbouring countries), to be yet another historical mistake.

The Duna Kor agrees with the opinion of the Presidium of the Hungarian Academy of Sciences, which in 1983 proposed to stop the project. We also agree with the 1985 proposal of the Academy to carry out an economic analysis before final decisionmaking. Environmental consequences, especially related to drinking water resources, should also be considered.

The Duna Kor will continue its work to protect the Danube. This Award will effectively help us, since we are going to spend the money to support environmental studies of the issue.

Judit Vasarhelyi (on behalf of Duna Kor)
9th December 1985

The Duna Kor, an informal group, originated from the winter months of 1984, when the question of the hydro-electric project was first taken up by the public. Open debates were held at universities, in colleges, and in local clubs of the official Patriotic Front, all of them attended by hundreds of people. Voices in scientific and professional circles, and in the literary world opposing the project, also became louder. The Presidium of the Hungarian Academy of Sciences suggested that the project be halted. Of the professional groups, it was the architects and engineers, influenced by technical as well as by moral motives, who took the lead. Their national association took an official stand against the project, which they have continued to maintain. Dozens of eminent writers, following an East-Central-European tradition of the literati being deeply concerned with the vital questions of the region, expressed their anxiety about the project. An open discussion, planned by the Association of Hungarian Writers, has however, been postponed due to political pressure. The public in Hungary has been more and more occupied with the problem. At the beginning of 1984 a group of students and intellectuals (biologists, architects, artists, historians, lawyers, sociologists, and teachers) initiated the foundation of an association for the protection of the Danube. The application for registration, however, has been blocked by the authorities. Nevertheless, those signing the application decided to collect and to publish information concerning the project, despite the ban. This activity had a special significance because a rigid ban, imposed on the publication of both pros and cons relating to the project, existed. The decision to ignore the ban made a breach in the information monopoly of the Hungarian water management authority. In the spring of 1984 a campaign to collect signatures was also launched. About ten thousand people had signed the petition by November, 1984, and demanded that the government should stop the work, and develop plans in accordance with environmental requirements. The petition has been left by the government, and by the Parliament, unanswered. Nevertheless, Duna Kor still insists upon the possibility of a dialogue.

Both spiritual and material values are endangered by the

project: the drinking water of millions; the landscape and nature; forests (like those in Hainburg); dozens of species of plants and animals; the Danube-bend, one of the most beautiful parts of our country, and historically important towns. Due to the complexity of what is to be protected, any critical activity must be based on several branches of science. The Duna Kor has its roots in a general process of mobilisation in society. Various strata, groups, and professional associations are striving for greater autonomy. More and more people wish that decisions concerning the present and future of small and large communities should be made, not behind closed doors, but openly based on social participation.

It is interesting and heartening to analyse the social backgrounds of those who signed the petition, or who attended the series of open discussions. Significantly a high number of manual workers, and of the rural population, are taking part in the initiative. The award of the Right Livelihood Foundation both reflects and enhances this democratic quality.

"The ordinary citizen cannot judge the scientific facts. What he can and must do is bring this reason and commonsense to bear on his country's whole approach to the problem", (Barbara Ward). During our activity we have been in a position to see that the number of such citizens, conscious of their responsibility, is increasing in Hungary every day. It is the opinions and beliefs of these citizens to which we would like to give voice. On their behalf, I consider it a great distincion to be able to express our thanks and gratitude to the Foundation for the prize awarded to Duna Kor.

NUCLEAR FREE ZONE IN PALAU
Chief Ibedul Yataka Gibbons
9th December 1983

IN OUR island tradition the role of a chief it to protect and provide; to reconcile and unify; and to lead and serve the interest of his people. This traditional role has been very much a part of an ever growing awareness and need for popular representation and participation. I stand before you in this capacity, to act for our people in receiving this award.

This occasion means so much to us. It means that small island nations are now recognized. It means that our struggle is no longer ours alone. It means that all people, all nations—big and small—should join their efforts now to work for a peaceful world, for a nuclear free world, for a world ruled not by alienation but by solidarity; a world ruled not by suspicion but by trust; a world ruled not by misery but by prosperity. The significance of the award for the republic of Palau cannot be over-emphasized.

Historical and Geographical.

Please allow me to explain where Palau is situated and why, in our view, this award is presented.

Palau is populated by nearly 15,000 people and located in the western end of the Pacific. These islands are abundantly blessed by nature. The air is always fresh and the sea is always clear. The skies are always blue during the day and starry during the night. The land is a lush green, still a paradise island as nature provided.

Historically, Palau was successively administered by Spain, Germany and Japan. Following the end of World War II under the United Nations Trusteeship Agreement, the United States was mandated to provide for the development of the political, social and economic well-being of the people of Palau and to rapidly return to Palau its rightful sovereignty over its own land.

In the early days, the ships that ushered in the forces of change also introduced amoeba and small-pox which greatly reduced the populations of the islands. More recently, the forces of World War II brought unimaginable human miseries. Destruction, death and displacement of our innocent people, and starvation, were everywhere. Traces of these are still visible today and Palau has not fully recovered from the effects of conventional warfare.

Following the end of World War II the hope for the end of misery came "by the dawns early light" when the United States began its administration of the islands. But our hopes turned into disillusionment. Our traditions became impaired and new concepts and ways were imposed upon us. The strategic aspect of the United States' military interests began to dominate our destiny. In the political status negotiations between Palau and the United States, the U.S. disclosed plans for Palau which included the use of nuclear and harmful substances. These plans became inseparable from the discussions relating to our long overdue decolonization.

The Struggle

I would like to take this opportunity to comment on the sharp conflict which now exists betyween Palau and the United States.

In 1980, Palau, at the urging of the United States, held a constitutional convention. The people of Palau drafted their first constitution of which we were very proud, because this was our first step towards self-determination.

The United States congratulated us. However, the United States had one very big problem. Palau adopted a constitution containing a nuclear ban which reads: "Harmful substances such as nuclear, chemical, gas or biological weapons intended for use in warfare, nuclear power plants and waste materials therefrom shall not be used, tested, stored or disposed of within the territorial jurisdiction of Palau without the expressed approval of not less than three-fourths (¾) of the votes cast in a referendum on this specific question."

Since the adoption of this nuclear ban, the United States has refused to envision a future political status in which the ban remains. The constitution of the republic of Palau reflects the history of the conflict between the desire of the people of Palau to maintain their home nuclear free, and the requirement of U.S. military interests. The framers of our constitution were well aware of the sufferings of the past, the miseries of warfare around the world and the threat of a holocaust in modern warfare. It was essential that a nuclear ban was woven into the drafting of the Palau constitution in 1979, which was adopted by a majority of 92% in a referendum. The constitution of Palau must survive.

On Februrary 10th, 1983, in a plebiscite, the people of Palau rejected a proposed Compact of Free Association with the United States, a Compact which would have governed Palau for many years. This Compact involved a new political status in which the United States would have removed Palau's nuclear ban. Despite initial claims to the contrary by the USA, the Compact of Free Association was declared dead by Palau's Supreme Court because it conflicted with our constitution. The United States now agrees with that court ruling.

In October of this year, in an attempt to resume negotiations toward decolonization, the leadership of Palau presented to the United States a new proposed Compact of Free Association which is in conformity with our constitution and expresses the legitimate needs of Palau. In Washington D.C. last month, the representatives of the United States informed Palau's leadership that in order for Palau and the United States to enter into any relationship of free association, Palau must lift its constitutional nuclear ban. This leaves my people with a very limited choice for their destiny—a continuation of colonialism under the United Nations trusteeship agreement or independence without adequate preparation and tools.

We regret the United States' objection to our constitution and particularly our nuclear ban. We understand that the United States believes it conflicts with U.S. military plans. But we have made it clear to the U.S. that Palau is not willing to be subjected to the testing and the use of nuclear substances, therefore taking the risk of being completely destroyed like our neighbours at Bikini Atoll in the Marshall Islands. We will continue to believe that a nuclear-free Palau is consistent with the interest of the United States to promote world peace.

CHAPTER TWO

People's Economics

People's Economics

IT IS becoming increasingly apparent that conventional economic wisdom is failing to develop solutions to the problems afflicting the world economy; in the West, large scale unemployment and inflation, in the Third World, mountainous national debts, and economic collapse manifested in the tragedies of disease, malnutrition, and starvation. In the tensions and conflicts which result, it is only the trade in weapons which prospers. Right livelihood depends on the emergence of new economic values and practices.

"The idea that there is an optimum size, a time to say 'enough', is still largely taboo, even though the only thing growing in our economies today is the social cost of growth, reducing our quality of life. Professor Leopold Kohr has shown that it is not our problems which are unprecedented, but their size: a return to a more human scale in our institutions and communities will make our problems manageable again. Even if we do not believe that smallness is always the answer, only by returning to a human scale will we be able to ask meaningful questions, and get any sensible answers at all".[1]

Leopold Kohr was born near Saltzburg, Austria, in 1909. In a wide ranging career which has taken him to all parts of the world, he has worked as a labourer in a Canadian goldmine, as a Republican journalist in the Spanish civil war, and as a lecturer at a succession of universities from Rutgers in the USA to Aberystwyth in Wales. As early as 1941 he had advocated the idea of a return to life in small communities organised on a human scale. Kohr attributes primary changes in history not to changes in religions or ideologies, nor to changing modes of production, but to changes in the size of society. His books, including 'The Breakdown of Nations' (1957), and 'The Over-Developed Nations' (1977) have been influential in promoting the attractions and viability of small scale organisation in political and economic systems.

Manfred A Max-Neef is a Chilean economist who founded, in 1981, the Centre for the Study and Promotion of Urban, Rural, and Development Alternatives (CEPAUR). The Centre was set up to deal with the problems caused by the phenomenon of hyper-industrialisation in the Third World, whereby the big cities expanded at such a fast pace that their growth has become unmanageable. Masses of people are drawn into the cities to face a future of unemployment in the sprawling squatter settlements. At the same time small cities and the rural communities stagnate and decay, and the human problems resulting from this consequence of centrally planned development present the poorer countries with a situation for which few viable solutions have been found. Manfred Max-Neef's work has been dedicated to the discovery of an alternative paradigm of development, which stimulates local self-reliance and satisfies human needs through a return to the human scale. His quest has not been merely a theoretical one. While challenging the assumptions of conventional development models, he has worked primarily on practical projects for alternative development. This work has been described by Max-Neef in his book 'From the Outside Looking In: Experiences in Barefoot Economics', where he provides an account of two of his experiences:

"The first is about the miseries of Indian and black peasants in the Sierra and coastal jungle of Ecuador. The second is about the miseries of craftsmen and artisans in a small region of Brazil . . . Both refer to a people's quest for self reliance. Both are lessons in economics as practised on a human scale".[2]

His speech in this section elaborates the principles and philosophy which guide his activities.

Pat Mooney and Cary Fowler have raised international awareness and understanding of an issue which lies at the heart of human biological and economic well-being, that is the preservation of the diversity of the world's agricultural gene pool. Mooney has been involved in development education for a number of years and has concentrated especially on agricultural and world food supply issues. He was involved with the World Food Conference of 1974 and later in the formation of the International Coalition for Development Action (ICDA). Through his association with Cary Fowler, who was working on the loss of agricultural genetic resources, Mooney turned his attention to this issue and published a report, 'Seeds of the Earth', in 1979.

Cary Fowler is currently Director of the Rural Advance-ment Fund and has acted as a consultant on food, agriculture, and development policy for a number of Canadian and international organisations. The work of Mooney and Fowler has highlighted the potential perils faced by the world's population by the reduction in genetic diversity in seed stocks, and the monopolisation of these by a small number of the Western based corporations and governments. The countries of the southern hemisphere, rich in genetic variety, have been donating germplasm in the belief that their botanical treasures form part of the common propery of humanity. Meanwhile, corporations based in the north have patented the offshoots of this heritage through plant breeding programmes, and have marketed the new seed stocks at great profit throughout the world.

The possibility of creatively linking common approaches to third world-first world problems is illustrated in the story of Erik Damman and the Future in Our Hands network. The Future in Our Hands movement started in 1974 in response to the publication of a book, carrying the same title, written by Erik Damman.[3] Damman had worked as a public relations consultant in Norway. Later, as the result of a period spent in Samoa, Damman began to feel that the material values dominating western societies formed one of the gravest dangers to mankind. By 1976, following the publication of his book in 1972, the movement had a membership of 20,000 in Norway, and it has since spread to Denmark and Sweden. The movement works for global justice, so that all may live as dignified human beings. To achieve this, people in the rich countries must themselves develop a new lifestyle where more value is attached to human than to material values, and the new lifestyle must involve a reduction in their levels of consumption. The movement believes that people will wish to free themselves from the materialistically dominated competition for goods. Reduced consumption can then create the opportunity to transfer resources to the poor, while changing at the same time the qualitative nature of relations between people in the materially affluent societies, promoting closeness, fellowship, and a sense of global responsibility.

Notes.

1. Jakob von Uexkull, Introductory Speech 1983

2. Manfred A Max-Neef, 'From the Outside Looking In: Experiences in Barefoot Economics', (1982).

3. See also E Damman, 'Revolution in the Affluent Society', (1979).

OVER DEVELOPMENT

Leopold Kohr

9th December 1983

IT IS a great honour to talk on the occasion of the
distribution of the Alternative Nobel Prize of 1983, on the
eve of what is bound to be one of the most fateful years of
history, George Orwell's 1984.

But there is always a chance that things might turn out
better than he envisioned. All that is necessary for our leaders
of both right and left is to let themselves be persuaded to
choose a third alternative to the ones offered by their
contrasting ideologies, but both hopelessly leading in the
same direction—the abyss of unmanageable proportions.
They are in a similar postition to the leaders of a boat floating
on the Niagara River which, having sprung a leak which its
capitalist crew is no longer able to mend, is taken over by a
socialist team whose unused energy and fresh approach has
the defect repaired in no time at all. Which seems splendid.
But, as I said, the boat is floating on the Niagara River. As a
result, what has so efficiently been fixed, causes the boat to be
sucked into the roaring abyss of the giant falls a few miles
lower down, all the faster precisely because it is so much fitter
than it was with its capitalist leak. The repair has provided
the same consolation to its occupants as a Welsh physician
said of the well medicated, ever jogging citizens of the United
States: they arrive on their deathbed in perfect shape. What
the occupants should have done is not repair the boat, but let

it sink, and swim to the nearest shore. That, not a change of ideology, would have been the saving alternative.

But what is the saving alternative for overcoming the difficulties confronting our political navigators? To give an answer, of which many are tendered, one must first know the question. What really is our main problem? Is it poverty? Is it hunger? Is it unemployment? Is it corruption, inflation, depression, juvenile delinquency? Is it the energy crisis? Is it war?

It is none of these. The real problem of our time is similar to the one besetting a mountain climber in the Himalayas. His heart aches, his lungs fail, his ears hurt, his eyes are blinded, his skin erupts, and yet, no heart, lung, ear, eye, or skin specialist can help, because there is nothing fundamentally wrong with either his organs or his skin.

His sole trouble is that he is too high up in the air. He suffers from altitude disease. And the answer is not to call in specialists, but bring him down to a lower level. Only if he still feels any of his pains at lower altitude does it make sense to call in a physician.

And so it is with the social diseases of our age. It is not poverty that is our problem. It is the vast spread of povery. It is not unemployment, but the dimension of modern unemployment, which is the scandal; not the hunger but the terrifying number afflicted by it; not depression but its world encircling magnitude; not war but the atomic scale of war. In other words, the real problem of our time is not material but dimensional. It is one of scale, one of proportion, one of size, not a problem of any particular system, ideology, or leadership. And, since the size of a social complexity takes its dimension from the society it afflicts, it follows that the only way of coping with it is, in analogy with the altitude disease, to bring the size of the afflicted society down to proportions within which man with his limited stature can once again assume control over it.

Even this will solve none of the problems bedevilling us.

The poor, as Jesus said 1950 years ago, will always be with us. "Men", as Hesiod said 2,800 years ago, in his story of the Box of Pandora—the collective gift of the Supreme Soviet of Divinities to the human species—"will go on destroying the cities of other men." And as my much admired late friend Howard Gossage of San Francisco liked to point out, 100 out of 100 will continue to die also in a small society. But the spectre of unmitigated, unending, uncopable horror, misery, and fear will wane along with their scale, until we are confronted with no more than the ordinary troubles fate has imposed on us as a moderator of the joys of our journey through life.

This amounts to an interpretation of history which assigns the determining influence on historic change not to such conventionally assumed causes as great leaders, religions, ideology, climate, topography, accident, or, as Marx has so brilliantly argued, to a change in the mode of production, but to the changing size of society. Mankind was expelled from Paradise not because Eve ate an apple, but because there were not enough apples left for the growing size of the population. Her sin was that she ate the last apple. This is why mankind had to earn henceforth its living with a harder mode of production—in the sweat of its brows. The symbolic signifcance of the story of the expulsion lies therefore, in the figleaf as the first means of birth control rather than in the apple as a Malthusian warning of the impending shortage of food supply due to an uninhibited rate of procreation.

And the same has been true all the way up to our present atomic mode of production. It is not nuclear power which has made it possible for the human population to increase; it is the other way round. As in all preceding industrial revolutions, the exploding human population has imposed on it the need of inventing an ever more efficient, this time an atomic, mode of production irrespective of whether it pollutes the air or leads to universal annihilation.

Beyond a critical social size, we simply cease to be masters of our destiny, or of the environment we have ourselves created. For as Theophrastus Paracelsus has said: "Everything is poison; it all depends on the quantity"—(Alles is Gift, ausschlaggebend ist nur die Menge.) This applies to mankind as much as to grasshoppers, who turned into a biblical plague merely by becoming too many. Or, to paraphrase Churchill's argument for the the reconstruction of Britain's House of Commons in its original small, dense, oblong form, encouraging debate rather than oratory as essential to the spirit of democracy ("we shape our buildings, but our buildings shape us"); so we may say of society that "we shape its size but its size shapes us."

For all this, the solution of the shortcomings of uncontrolled free capitalism lies therefore no longer, as it once might have been, in an increase of coordination and socialist controls. For the leadership of neither the one nor the other of our alternative social ideologies can exercise control over what has outgrown all human control, because of the excessive size of our integrated political and economic environment.

Nor does the solution lie in the union of peoples or nations. This would simply make the problem of excessive size even larger than it already is. For our difficulties are not the result of division imposed on us by our blasphemous attempts at unification in the Towers of Babel and Manhattan, but of bad division resulting from the unequal national size, in which the parts of the human race have organized themselves through a process of lopsided regional unification.

The primary problems thus being ones of excessive size, of unsurveyable dimensions, of cancerous overgrowth and unstable bigness, the only practical solution must logically lie not in still larger units which increase all their problems, in proportion to their enlarged scale, but in the opposite direction: in smallness. This alone can solve the host of secondary problems which are mere offshoots of the primary problem of excessive social size. And it solves them, not by their abolition, but by making them manageable through the reduction of their scale.

This was done politically in the successful cantonal structures of federal and confederal enterprises, reaching from the continental expanse of the Holy Roman Empire, down to small Switzerland, and up again to the United States, and demonstrating that even a major union can manage the problems of scale as long as its divided subordinate parts are all equally (or even unequally) small. Militarily it was demonstrated by the Truce of God during the Middle Ages, through the strategem of splitting the actions of belligerents. It wisely never prohibited war. All it did was to cut it down to bearable proportions. It permitted it on weekdays, but never on Sundays, Saturdays, and Saints Days, of which there were a peace-insuring plentitude. However, the real reason that caused the lusty warriors to adhere to its restrictions was less their piety than the physical fact that they were all too small to contradict the moral authority of a Church which was not too powerful either. But in a system of small bishoprics and states, it had a critical superiority even over its strongest subordinate units most of the time. This is not theory, but the arithmetic of submission. Only when Emperor Maximillian, the first modern illusionist, promulgated the Eternal Truce of God in an attempt to transform the fragmentized insignificant splinter wars into a condition of indivisible peace, did this horse sense design fail, providing the world with the spectacle of two bloody indivisible wars per century ever since.

For all this, the answer to the overriding problem of bigness is therefore not socialism, capitalism, fusionism, or pacifism, as it is constantly preached—to no avail. The answer to the problem of bigness is smallness. For to stress again, the primary cause of human misery is no longer ideology, religion, political division or economic system, but excessive size. And if smallness is the answer it is not only because it is beautiful, as Fritz Schumacher phrased it so fetchingly in a bestseller which is praised by many but followed by few. The reason why it is beautiful is that it is also natural, in harmony with the scheme of things or, to cite the title of the book by another old friend living in little Liechtenstein, Josef Haid: it is *Lebensrichtig* which, translated into English, expresses the same fundamental idea as the Right Livelihood Foundation.

Lebensrichtig, (or right livelihood) is indeed the basic strength of the argument for smallness. It is the building principle of the universe in all its manifestations—physical, mathematical, chemical, musical, biological, architectural, medical, economic, political, and social.

In chemistry it has inluenced the studies which led Peter Mitchell to a Nobel Prize in 1978. In economics it was expressed by men such as Raul Prebish in what he called the Law of Peripheral Neglect; and by another Nobel Prize winner, Gunnar Myrdal, in his Theory of Circular and Cumulative Causation, in which he demonstrated the retarding rather than beneficial effect of big common markets on its less advanced members. And Erwin Schrodinger, a winner of the Nobel Prize in Physics has shown in a delightful booklet 'What is Life', not only that atoms are small, which everybody knows, but answered the all-important question, why they are small. Existing in vast numbers, and moving perpetually in unrestrained freedom, they are statistically bound to clash in ever recurring collisions. Were they large, or interspersed with large ones like cancer cells are in the human body—(or Big Powers in the body politic), their collisions would inevitably result in destruction. However, being small, their collisions, like those of dancing couples in a ballroom, are not only harmless but create a never ending chain of new constellations, forms and order, by releasing with each disturbance themselves the forces leading to a new equilibrium. They interact like the delicate mobiles hanging over the desks of various executives, and, ensuring with their gentle movements caused by every breath of air, a landscape not of turmoil but of soothing peace—without government, without direction, and without control. In a universe of small parts, there is no need of an adjusting hand, not even of the Creator, who shaped the world to be a satisfied spectator rather than a tirelessly intervening watchdog.

In philosophy, the most eloquent of the early defenders of smallness as a cure for our social ills was Aristotle, who considered the ideal state as one that can be taken in at a single view, and in which everything can be solved because the connections are transparent; all is translucent, and nothing can stay hidden. I was reminded of this when I asked Prime Minister Alexander Frick of Liechtenstein in 1945, whether his tiny country, like such giants as the United Kingdom, France, China, Italy, Germany or Japan, required American aid. "Look," was his answer with a touch of hurt pride: "Why on Earth should we need aid? By the time a big power learns of a disaster, we in Liechtenstein are half way through mending the damage." And when I asked two weeks ago a Liechtenstein postmaster what he considered to be his problem, he instantly answered: "none". This was concurred in by his wife, though not quite shared by another former Prime Minister, Dr. Gerard Batliner who, nearly 40 years after Alexander Frick, confessed to some apprehension at the slowly growing trend among his country's younger generation to expand their commercial involvements beyond the limits of visibility and influence, in response to the lures of the vast reaches of the Common Market and a more interdependent world community. For bigness is not only bad. It is also very contagious and, alas, satanically attractive—like hell which, in the end produces the greatest terror afflicting all living things—fear.

Saint Augustine, another of the early great apostles of smallness, asked the Romans after pointing at the fragilty of big states; "What reason or what wisdom shall any man show in glorying in the largeness of empire, all their joy being but a glass, bright and brittle, and evermore in fear and danger of breaking? "As a result, he suggested, as one must again suggest today, that, in the terms of Neville Figgis' summary, "the world would be most happily governed if it consisted not of a few aggregations secured by wars of conquest, with their accompaniment of despotism and tyrannical rule, but of a society of small states, living together in amity, not transgressing each other's limits, unbroken by jealousies."

But Saint Augustine did not only preach the idea of smallness along lines proposed by many other realistic appraisers of human nature (whom we are wont to call utopians), such as Plato, Thomas More, Campanella, Fourier. Like Robert Owen, the founder of the Co-operative Movement (which flourishes in the individuality of its autonomous small units to this day), Saint Augustine also put the idea to practical use by laying the foundation of those monasteries whose extent, like John Seymour's self-sufficient farms, was limited by definition to their immediate neighbourhood. Their vita communis has paradoxically provided the world with the root of the term communism which, grown into giantism, inspires as much terror as its capitalist countervailing giant whom it tries to combat, proving once again that Paracelsus' dictum: "everything is poison; it all depends on the quantity", applies even to Saint Augustine's gentle monastic communism.

It is therefore not union, capitalism, or socialism, but the return to a properly divided cantonal, Augustinian monastic, or Owenite co-operative network of small cells, loosely linked together as in a religious order spanning the world, which offers the chance, as it did throughout the ages, of, among many other things, successfully raising the standards of underdeveloped regions. For it makes it possible to develop them not with aid as perpetually dependent, alienated ill-tempered frustrates bearing no gratitude for their assisters, but without aid—as independent, glittering communities reaching prosperity, security, and contentment infinitely faster than is now possible under the centralized direction of distant benefactors. All that is required is to use intensively the material and intellectual resources of their immediate neighbourhood. For this is the only way of saving, as Henry Charles Carey has called it, "the heaviest tax on land and labour—the cost of transportation," which mounts geometrically with every arithmetical increase in distance, impoverishing the standard and quality of life through the very help tendered to improve them.

True unassisted development means a return also to what Schumacher called Intermediate Technology, (that is, working longer and harder). But working longer and harder is exactly what a world needs which has been pushed into ever mounting unemployment and idleness by the Advanced Technology, of the sort so bitingly illustrated by Charlie Chaplin in his film Modern Times. However, if Intermediate Technology is to provide the same high living standard as Advanced Technology, it must, of necessity, be applied to areas and societies of limited extent. For only within small social environments is Intermediate Technology not only appropriate, adequate and economical but more economical than even the most Advanced Technology, just as a row boat is more economical when crossing the Thames than a jet.

This is why, concentrating their energies on the cultivation of their immediate environment, ancient and medieval monasteries were able to contract out of their crumbling surrounding empires maintained by a venial bureaucracy, serving an impotent government apparatus. Instead they could build, as Toynbee would say, "away from all distraction" and government guidance, the glittering network of practically sovereign communities, in a time which it takes modern engineers of large-scale living to prepare merely their pre-investment infra-structures. With water, wind and muscle power, they developed husbandry, agriculture, forests and fisheries in such amplitude, that fast days, (when only fish was allowed), accompanied by such appropriate monastic by-products as Benedictine and Chartreuse, became feast days joyfully looked forward to. And when their material needs had been locally provided for, the monks began to adorn their cells with immortal paintings, compose music for their prayers, educate the young in Latin and Greek, sponsor literature, architecture, and the arts, and copy in illuminated letters the authors of antiquity on enduring parchment, without which the roots of Western civilisation would have vanished without a trace.

They make one understand how the city states of antiquity, freed of Carey's "tax" of transportation and haulage cost from far away, were able to build, as the Athenians did with the Acropolis, in a single generation the structures of which the geographer Pausanias said centuries later: "When they were new, they looked already ancient: now that they are old, they still look new."

Similar principles enabled Philip II of Spain to develop the enchanting regional city-state pattern of Mexico, by the simple device of decreeing that monasteries must be located so far apart from each other (and in particular from the pleasures of Mexico City), that it was too difficult for them to waste their time in incessant communication—the very opposite of contemporary development planning by academic chumming. This left them with no alternative but to duplicate autonomously in rival splendour what they could not enjoy by touring the already developed centres far away.

And even in our own time, similarly successful development experiments were undertaken by the Amish and Mennonites in both North and South America, the Kibbutz communities of Israel, and by the small rural communes of communist China which so impressed the late great Joan Robinson of Cambridge that she unwittingly embraced the teachings of John Seymour of County Wexford in Ireland. The Chinese development device for local communes was not the extension of government control and aid beyond the measure of a birthday gift, but by withdrawing what could not have been offered anyway, and encouraging instead the idea that the locals should do things locally with the tools, however, primitive, they already had. For pyramids, cathedrals, factories, roads are, in the last analysis, not built by money or machinery (which is scarce even in the richer countries, considering that they can never get enough of it), but by hands, which are ample even in the poorest communities, and represent the only alternative energy source which can never be exhausted because everybody is born with it.

But once again, for the intermediate technology of muscle power to be economical, the society served by it must be small, as I can see every day in my alternative little home town of Aberystwyth in Wales, where I can achieve more on foot, which costs nothing, than by car, which costs a lot, and with which I can do nothing at all except leave town.

So, let us solve the one insoluble problem of our time, the high-altitude disease of excessive size and uncontrollable proportions, by going back to the alternative to both right and left, that is to a small-scale social environment with all its potential for global pluralist co-operation and largely unaffiliated self sufficiency. This may be achieved by extending not centralized control, but by decontrolling locally centred and nourished communities, (each with its own nuclear institution and a limited but strong and independent gravitational field) as it existed in the case of medieval monasteries and convents. Their abbots, sisters and brothers will then be able to provide the world, once again, with the guidance, understanding, humanity and taste it needs.

But smallness is the only way that is natural, sound, lebensrichtig, practical, scientific, and beautiful on top of it. What does not work, as everyone should know by now, is bigness, unification, integration, international hymn-singing, handholding and loquacious conferencing in which all those believe who hold the reins of power in their hands, and actually could do something with it other than guiding us to the nuclear terminus.

The alternative is to dissolve overgrown human aggregations, before they reach the critical mass at which they explode spontaneouly. Which of course is a solution, too. It is in fact nature's own alternative, which it applies whenever it gets tired of a system. Then it kills it off by letting it overgrow until it either explodes or collapses into itself.

This spectre of collapse by overgrowth should make the solution of smallness a little more palatable, just as a Sunday sermon picturing hell should make the heavenly blessings of sinlessness a little bit more appealing than they usually are. But there is always the argument that smallness is just the irrational dream of a romantic. Of course it is romantic. But only to a romantic does life make sense. Starting from nothing, and ending in nothing, and costing a lot of money in between, is rationally and economically an indefensible loss proposition.

Only a romantic sees glory and meaning in the rainbow spanning the two zero magnitudes which mark the beginning and the end.

And it is also said that in this age of progress it makes no sense to step back. To which the great Welsh anthropologist Alwyn Rees used to reply: "When one has reached the edge of the abyss, the only thing that makes sense is to step back".

The confrontation of our age is not between capitalism and communism, left and right, man and woman, black and white, young and old. These are the issues of the past, lingering on like the glow of the sun after it has set. The real confrontation of our age is man versus mass, the individual versus society, the citizen versus the state, the small community versus the big one, David versus Goliath. As Andre Gide said on his death bed:"I love small nations. I love small numbers. The world will be saved by the few": George Orwell permitting!

BAREFOOT ECONOMICS

Manfred Max-Neef

9th December 1983

SINCE, in the note on the presentation of the award to me, reference is made to my being a "barefoot economist", I should devote some minutes to the story of my metamorphosis. It all began—as I have told it in my book 'From the Outside looking In'—when I went through a deep personal crisis as an economist. At a certain stage, almost two decades ago, I realized that economists had become dangerous people. Their discipline—(despite Lord Keynes warning to the effect that the importance of economic problems should not be overestimated, with the result that matters of higher and more permanent significance are sacrificed to its supposed necessities)-suddenly became *the* magic science: the one to provide the answers to most of the pressing problems affecting humanity. Its practitioners, newly endowed with this unexpected power to exercise their influence over enterprises, interest groups and governments, swiftly and proudly took for granted their new role as inaccessible and powerful sorcerers. It soon followed that economics, originally the offspring of moral philosophy, lost a good deal of its human dimension, to see it replaced by fancy theories and technical trivialities that are incomprehensible to most and useful to none, except to their authors who sometimes win prizes with them.

After a number of years the enthusiasm and optimism

with which I had worked as an economist for several international organizations gave way to a growing uneasiness. To continue being engaged, whether as a witness or as a direct participant, in efforts to *diagnose poverty*, to *measure* it and to *devise indicators* in order to set up a statistical or conceptual threshold beyond which a percentage may reveal the numerical magnitude of those to be classified as the extremely poor; and then to participate in costly seminars and even costlier conferences in order to communicate the findings, interpret the meaning of the findings (my God!!), criticize the methodologies behind the findings, express our deep concern (often during cocktails) for what the findings show. Finally to end up with recommendations to the effect that what must urgently be done is to allocate more funds for further research into the subject, to be discussed again in other meetings—made me feel at a certain point that I was happily participating in a rather obscene ritual.

Furthermore my awareness about the fact that I was living in a world in which, despite all kinds of transcendental conferences, accumulated knowledge and information, grand economic and social plans and 'development decades', increasing proverty—both in relative as well as in absolute terms—is as indisputable a statistical trend as it is an obvious and conspicuous fact to anyone just willing to look around and *see*, induced me to re-evaluate my role as an economist. The critical exercise—to put it in a nutshell—led me to the identification of four areas of personal concern: our unlimited admiration for giantism and 'big' solutions; our obsession with abstract measurements and quantifiers; our mechanistic approach to the solution of economic problems; and our tendency to oversimplify, as reflected by our efforts to favour an assumed 'technical objectivity' at the expense of losing a moral vision, a sense of history and a feeling for social complexity.

It is only fair to say the *some* economists were not afflicted by the malady. My contacts with a few of them proved to be decisive, inasmuch as the conclusions I drew from the critical incursions into which I ventured under their influence were enough to change the course of my life, not only as a professional, but as a human being as well.

I must say that I am extremely happy that one of those truly great economists—one whom I have always considered as the 'Maestro'—is also being honoured today: Professor Leopold Kohr from Austria.

Well, it so happened that I severed my ties with the trends imposed by the economic establishment, disengaged myself from 'objective abstractions' and decided to 'step into the mud'. Thus I became, and still remain, a 'barefoot economist'.

I could tell you stories of what I have done in the past, but I shall refrain from doing so. Since I interpret this award not as the coronation of a life work, but as a stimulus to continue along the path I have chosen, I shall refer to the challenges peoples and groups like us—the awardees— are facing in the future as I see it.

Let me start with a general diagnosis.

Three decades in which a technocratic, mechanistic and top-down development paradigm has been predominant have produced a kind of global crisis that has no precedent in history. The characteristics of the crisis, as it affects the Third World, can be synthetized in terms of a disturbing paradox: that the utmost absurdity may be—and in most cases already is—that the economic benefits accruing from the dominant development model are used in the solution of those acute problems and contradictions created by the same development model. In short, a self-defeating process: the serpent devouring its own tail.

In almost any Third World country, we may grossly divide the population into two main groups. Firstly, those people who are directly or indirectly linked to a 'development strategy' and, secondly, those people—most often the majority—who are left to design their own 'survival strategy'.

The fact that both groups still coexist the world over and that, furthermore, the increase of the latter group is indisputable, should be proof enough that the mechanistic possibilities of the so called 'trickle down effect' originally attributed to global development models, did not work.

The accumulated experience and frustrations have allowed for an alternative development paradigm to surface. Generally identified as the bottom-up approach, although much older than the former—it has only in recent years gained sufficient 'respectability' to become the object of increasing attention among experts, policy makers and the concerned public in general. The 1975 'What Now' Dag Hammarskjold Report, while proclaiming the urgency as well as the philosophy for 'Another Development', was a decisive step in raising public and specialized consciousness with respect to the need to unleash new processes where the overriding goals of development and equity might truly converge. Yet we must be careful because, at this point, we are standing at a cross-roads. If the orthodox paradigm generated development without equity, the new one should escape the risk of turning into a promoter of equity without development. Furthermore, it should be kept in mind that paradigms can be dangerous, especially if they become 'fashionable'. Slogans must not replace facts and evidence, and emotions must not overrun the hard work necessary to construct a solid and coherent humanistic theory.

If understood as an alternative process, the new emerging paradigm can be envisaged, at this stage, as a chain with several loose links. As a body in search of its consolidation it still leaves much to be desired. We do know the body's principal components, but we still don't know how they are supposed to interrelate for the whole to function harmoniously. A return to the human scale, active and creative public participation, satisfaction of fundamental human needs, ecological constraints, local self reliance; these are some of its basic goals. Size of systems (or critical systems size) and efficiency as a quality (not quantity) are two of its parameters. Subversion of centralized power and authority, of bureaucratic structures, of mechanistic models and of other technocratic instrumentalities are cornerstones of its philosophico-political foundations. The heart seems to be in the right place. All the pieces seem to be there. The grand question is how to put them all together.

If we reflect about the essence of both paradigms, we may conclude that the former, being essentially simple, has been artificially complicated. The new one, being essentially complex and sensitive, is running the risk of being artificially oversimplified. Evidences of the latter are already at work. In fact, one sometimes gets the impression, when discussing with adherents to the new alternative, that a frequent belief seems to be that promoters and activists alone can take care of the entire process. One remains with the sensation that an aspired stronger focus on practical aspects often seems to imply an aspired stronger focus on the disengagement from the thinker. Such a situation is dangerous. It reveals the existence of potential seeds of self-destruction that this paradigm—as every paradigm—carries within itself. If those incipient seeds are not promptly sterilized, and the already emerging malaise is not urgently cured, the new paradigm— its indisputable merits notwithstanding—may decay before having had the chance of proving its worthiness. The risk, right now, is real. Hence, one should keep in mind that action alienated from theory is as dangerous as theory alienated from reality. Theory and praxis are both indispensable; none can substitute for each other. While practitioners and promoters of alternative processes are legion already, the number of those dedicated to the systematization of accumulated knowledge and experiences is small. Moreover, those few groups who are dedicated to the task work mostly in isolation and are, hence, devoid of the benefits of cross-fertilization that a dynamic network of horizontal communication can bring about.

However important the systematization towards the construction of a coherent humanistic alternative theory (or theories) may be, it is only a part of the problem to be solved. The fact remains that both paradigms will—and most probably must—continue to coexist even if in a dialectical struggle with one another. Continued coexistence seems to be inevitable for the simple reason that the macro is not the sum of the micro processes, nor can the latter be interpreted as the disaggregation of the former. Both processes are interdependent rather than independent. How such an interdependence may be rationally articulated is the second part of the problem to be solved. In short, the situation—and the challenge—may be summarized as follows: while the many deficiencies and limitations of the theory that supports the old paradigm must be overcome (mechanistic interpretations and inadequate indicators among others), a theoretical body for the new paradigm must still be constructed. But let me make it very clear—I could not stress this point enough—that I am not advocating theory for the sake of theorizing. Of that we have had enough! What I am proposing instead is the coherent systematization of the experience acquired by all those of us who have been working for years in the alternative solutions of the real problems affecting our world today; especially the poorest and most vulnerable sectors of humanity.

All those of us—and we are many indeed—who have put their efforts in the search for more humane development alternatives, share common goals and common philosophical principles. Yet we still don't share a common language. The construction of that language through solid theoretical contributions, based—and only based—on our concrete experiences, is one of the great tasks we must yet fulfil.

But let me say at this point that whatever tasks we are facing, the tools from which we may choose to carry out our labour are part of a culturally impoverished environment. Of an environment in which the cultural wealth of diversity and variety has been substituted by the economic efficiency of monotony and uniformity. In order to illustrate my point I shall refer to the cultural impoverishment brought about by the economically dominated developmental process. Let me simply refer to language.

In its widest sense, language is the product as well as the representation of a culture. To the extent that it grows or diminishes, becomes enriched or impoverished, the same occurs with the culture to which it belongs and which it represents. As our language expands in the direction demanded by an increasingly technocratic culture, its rhetorical possibilities for the eloquent exaltation and presentation of alternative cultural routes becomes atrophied. If we consider it appropriate to refer to development in terms of figures and quantities, then figures and quantities will make up the language of development, which in turn implies that what remains outside that language remains outside of our development. Now it should be clear that if the language used is poor, incomplete and insufficient, the development will also be poor, incomplete and insufficient. We have become so fascinated with numbers, and so obsessed with quantifiers, in our ludicrous effort to construct a value-free economic development theory, that in our over-enthusiasm we no longer realize that we have turned logic upside-down. In fact, instead of learning how to interpret what is really important, we grant importance only to that which can be measured. We should not be surprised, therefore, that probably nothing is more important than income which, according to our development language, is the measure of measures. If our language knows how to measure income better than most quantifiers, we should venerate such quantifiers above many other considerations. Development is measured by income, well-being becomes a function of income, inflation is income wrongly generated, and unemployment is income not generated. Just like that, all cut and dried.

The fact that many of us insist that development is something more, and that inflation is something less, and that well-being implies some transcendental things, and that unemployment is many tragedies with name and face, with anguish and pain; this seems to have no echo in systems whose discourse is based on the assumed solidity and strength of abstract and dehumanized statistics. This makes us, who search for more humane alternatives, a humanistic subset of a technocratically dehumanized set. In trying to enrich and improve our language, we become the victims of a hostile environment in which the impoverished language is the language of power, of greed and of domination.

No matter how hostile the environment in which we are working is, we must never cease to insist that development is about people and not about objects. That the aim of development must be neither producerism nor consumerism but the satisfaction of fundamental human needs, which are not only needs of *having* but needs of *being* as well. We will never deny that subsistence is a fundamental human need, which must be satisfied through adequate income, nutrition, housing and work for all. But we will also insist that protection, affection, understanding, participation, leisure, creation, identity and freedom are extremely fundamental human needs as well.

Our impoverished development models have been mainly concerned with subsistence. But dominated as such models are by the religion of economic efficiency and the magic of the market, they have over-saturated the satisfaction of some at the expense of the misery of the majority of mankind. And what about the rest of the fundamental human needs? Well, our dominant models work nicely and very efficiently against their satisfaction.

What *protection* can we talk about in the midst of growing militarization and the arms race? What *affection* can grow under the prevalence of patriarchal and authoritarian structures? How can true human *understanding* grow under the prevalence of patriarchal and authoritarian structures? How can true human *understanding* grow from educational systems disengaged from the real problems of the world? How can we talk of *participation* where women, minorities and even majorities are discriminated against? What *leisure* can be meaningful where silly gadgets and an alienating electronic media bombard us day and night? How can human *creativity* really flourish where, for the sake of economic efficiency, people who are potentially creative subjects are turned into efficient objects? And what about *identity* in a world full of political exiles, and of groups who have to suffer the imposition of means and ways that are alien to their culture?

And *freedom?* Where is *freedom?* It has gone into hiding because it wants to survive. It shows us its face here and there, like in this corner called Sweden that is awarding a group of crazy but very active romantics today. We know where it hides, and we shall never tell the enemy. But in the meantime we will carry on our work. We will recover the wealth of our language, and give meaning again to what is really meaningful, and call all things and actions by their real name.

All those of us—and let me repeat that we are many— who work at the human scale for *human* solutions where human beings really *are,* form a group that is powerful because it lacks all greed for power. We are—like in ancient times of generalized crisis—the new 'monasteries' where the wealth of our cultural variety and diversity shall be preserved, until the hordes of uniformity, of power, of depletion and of greed collapse under the unsustainable weight of their own gigantic stupidity.

I call on Goethe's Faust, for him to tell us that: 'Die Kunst ist lang, das Leben kurz' (Art is long and life is short). Let us, through our deeds, remain always as parts of art, and in that manner help life to remain on the earth!

AGRICULTURAL HERITAGE

Cary Fowler and Pat Mooney*

9 December 1985

SOMETHING strange and wonderful began to happen 12000 years ago. People began to make the transition from being hunters and gatherers to being farmers. They began to plant and care for the seeds they once gathered. Thus our Stone Age ancestors—mostly the women—initiated the process of domesticating the plants that would become the crops we depend on today.

Virtually all of our major food crops originated in the Third World: wheat and barley in the Near East; soybeans and rice in China; sorghum and yams in Africa; maize, potatoes and tomatoes in Latin America.

Over the last 12000 years these crops have had to adapt to countless environmental conditions—different soils and climates, pests and diseases. Barley, for example, had to adapt not only to growing in Ethiopia, but to growing in Sweden. The result of this history has been thousands of distinct varieties of barley, wheat, rice, maize and other crops—each genetically distinct, each adapted to a certain set of conditions. This diversity, found mainly in the Third World, is the legacy of the past 12000 years. These are the genetic resources that constitiute the very foundation of agriculture.

It is customary and appropriate when receiving an award such as this to thank one's family, close friends and colleagues. We wish to do that. Without their help we could have done very little. And we must recognize the work of some of the great pioneering scientists in this field: N. I. Vavilov, Jack Harlan, Erna Bennett, and T. T. Chang. Our modest achievements would look small if compared to theirs. But most of all we recognize the achievements of millions of anonymous people—your ancestors and mine who created the genetic diversity that gives life to agriculture and to us.

But this genetic diversity is being lost. The foundation of agriculture is shattering. New varieties are replacing traditional varieties. And the traditional varieties are becoming extinct. The same process is underway with livestock breeds. In the United States we cultivated over 7000 named varieties of apples in the last century. Over eighty five per cent (more that 6000) are now extinct. When I give lectures back home I often pass out a list of these extinct apples, and I say look for your family names on this list. It was your ancestors who developed these varieties and often they gave them the highest honor they could—they gave them their names. Two-thirds of an audience in the U.S. will find family names on this list of extinct apple varieties. It is a powerful testament to the loss of our own history and culture, as well as to the loss of characteristics and qualities that will never be seen again. Increasingly this loss of diversity means that we are losing not just the actors in this drama but some of the roles as well.

When we talk about traditional varieties and rare breeds disappearing, we are really talking about extinction—the permanent loss of genes—sometimes the very genes plant or animal breeders need now, or may need a hundred years from now, to rescue a crop from a disease or adapt the crop to new human needs. The loss of genetic diversity limits the evolution and development of agricultural crops. It narrows and eliminates options for the future.

In the 1840s a terrible potato blight struck Ireland. None

of the potatoes that had found their way from their homeland in the Andes Mountains to Ireland were resistant to the blight. The potatoes died and so did over a million people. Over a million more emigrated to the New World, including Pat's ancestors and mine. Fortunately resistance to this blight still existed amongst the potatoes in the Andes. If it did not, we would not be able to eat potatoes today. The crop simply would not exist.

But if another blight suddenly and unexpectedly strikes potatoes, will we find the needed diversity in the Andes this time? If we have to go back to the Near East in order to save wheat from a similar fate, what will we find?

These are not theoretical questions. In recent years barley and rice have been saved by finding just the primitive variety that had the needed resistance. Tomatoes, sugarcane and tobacco have been salvaged as crops by using genes from their wild relatives. We have come very close to major catastrophies. We may in fact be experiencing such catastrophies now with the coffee crop in Latin America, with citrus canker in the U.S. and with African Swine Fever.

Naturally we in industrialized countries talk of the need to preserve genetic diversity for its possible benefit to our own crops. Our scientists say we will need certain qualities—disease resistance or drought tolerance—some day. But that day has already arrived in much of the Third World, where farmers cannot afford the imported fertilizers and pesticides to put on modern varieties, or the fancy confinement barns some modern hog breeds require. In the Third World, millions of lives depend not just on the yield of the crops but on the reliability of that yield. The tragic situation of Ethiopia bears witness to that fact. Ethiopia is officially the poorest country in the world. It will not be able to feed its people using crop varieties that require steady supplies of water or expensive imported fertilizers and pesticides. In fact, the use of such varieties in Ethiopia has killed people. Instead, Ethiopia will have to depend on crops adapted to the harsh conditions found in Ethiopia. The prerequisite of this is saving Ethiopia's wealth of genetic resources. If these resources are lost, building a sustainable, self-reliant system of agriculture in Ethiopia will be nearly impossible. And Ethiopia's famine will be a permanent famine.

When traditional varieties become extinct, communities lose a bit of their history and culture. The plant species loses a bit of its gene pool. Future generations lose some of their options, and the present generation forfeits its self-reliance. The type of seed sown to a large extent determines the farmer's need for fertilizers and pesticides. It influences the need for machinery and often dictates the market for the crop . . . and the ultimate consumer. Communities that lose traditional varieties adapted over centuries to their needs lose control and become dependent, forever, on outside sources of seeds and the chemicals needed to grow and protect them. Without an agricultural system adapted to a community and its environment, self-reliance in agriculture is impossible. Saving agriculture's diversity does not guarantee self-reliance or development. But losing this diversity does narrow the options and foster dependency.

Since the days of Vavilov in the Soviet Union, massive collections of crop genetic diversity in the form of seeds have been assembled and placed in gene banks for preservation. But the promise of gene banks to preserve genetic diversity may never be fulfilled. Despite the dedication and hard work of the scientists involved, large collections have been and are being lost. As Jack Harlan has said, if we are willing to entrust the fate of mankind to these collections, we are living in a fool's paradise.

Extinction is a process, not simply an event that occurs when the last individual of a species dies. Extinction is a process that happens as a plant or animal species loses the ability to evolve. Therefore conservation of plants and animals implies retaining the ability to evolve. And that means saving the stuff that makes evolution and change possible—genetic diversity.

Increasingly we are drawn to the conclusion that if genetic diversity is to be saved it will be saved by the people who created it in the first place—the world's farmers and gardeners. Their interest in and love of this diversity will last longer than governments themselves. In their fields the agricultural legacy of thousands of years can continue to co-evolve with the environment.

So to governments we say—recognise the importance of individual action. Encourage it. Work with it. Understand that the best system for conserving genetic resources includes both gene banks and farmers.

And to individuals we say—recognize that the job is big and costly and that we will not be successful if we do not convince our governments to participate actively and constructively in genetic conservation work.

To preserve genetic diversity we must engage in both conservation and politics. As the only species ever powerful enough to affect all evolution on this planet, this is our responsibility. If we fail, the genetic heritage of 12000 years will disappear in the next twelve.

Agriculture is 12000 years old, but in human history it is a recent development. Ninety percent of all human beings who ever lived on earth were hunters and gatherers. Only six percent have been farmers.

Mark Twain once said something that I think helps tie this history to the present crisis involving genetic diversity. He said that the first rule of successful tinkering is to save all the pieces. When it comes to agriculture, our history makes us just tinkerers, not experts. If we are to be successful tinkerers, we must become the people who save all the pieces.

The fact that pieces are beginning to disappear, or that actors and whole roles in the agricultural pageant have begun to vanish, first became apparent and a problem for the industrialized countries.

Europe and North America had their green revolution

much earlier in this century. The old seeds have almost all been replaced by new high-response varieties. Northern scientists, aware that the genes are the first link in the food chain, and that the collection and conservation of crop diversity is a matter of vital national security, have launched hundreds of collection missions in the fields of Asia, Africa and Latin America. As a result, more than two-thirds of collected genetic diversity is stored in gene banks in Europe and North America. In a handful of seedy Fort Knoxes in the United States, the Soviet Union, Japan and Italy and a few other countries, are stored the world's most valuable raw material.

Yet it is a raw material unlike any other in the world. It has not been bought. It has been donated. It has been donated by the poor to the rich. The donation has been made under a noble banner proclaiming that genetic resources form a part of the common heritage of all humanity and thus can be owned by no one.

But as the primary building block of agriculture, genes have incalculable political and economic importance. Industrialized governments—often overruling the intentions of their scientists—have come to hoard germplasm and to stock seeds as part of the arsenal of international power diplomacy. Private companies in the North—although glad to receive free genes—are loath to divulge or share the adaptions they draw from these donations.

The issue has arisen at the United Nations Food and Agriculture Organization, where Third World countries have questioned the logic of the flow of their botanical treasures to the North, and have challenged the economic sense of volunteering profits to private interests. You will remember the debate over the Law of the Sea, where the world said that the seabed should be the common heritage of all humanity and some countries in the North said, 'no, let's see who gets there first.' Now these same Northern states, looking into the fields and forests of the South, are saying that this raw material should be uniquely the common heritage of all humanity.

In the last few years the gene donor countries in the South have had increased cause for concern. During the grain embargo of the Soviet Union, Canada and the United States also instituted a gene embargo. Last year a Sino-American trade dispute led to a disruption of germplasm exchanges between those countries. Also last year an effort was made to exclude socialist countries of southern Africa from benefitting from a sorghum and millet germplasm development program in the region. This year a trade embargo of Nicaragua also includes a gene embargo, including the seed which Nicaraguan farmers have donated and entrusted for safe-keeping in the North. This is not just. This is not Right Livelihood.

It is not surprising that the control of a scarce resource has become politicized. In fact it is more surprising that those countries that have absorbed the lion's share of collected diversity now claim that there is no political problem.

Neither is it surprising that the implications of genetic wipe-out have attracted considerable commercial interest. More than a decade ago, international chemical companies observed that the green revolution showed that it is possible to market a single crop variety over thousands of kilometers of land, and that with the help of foreign aid and government subsidies poor farmers could be an easy market for expensive seed. Chemical companies also noted the potential value of Third World genes as the cornerstone of genetic engineering, and they applauded the opportunity to obtain exclusive monopoly control over seeds through national patent legislation. In the dozen years since, more than 900 family seed companies have become controlled or taken over by major enterprises. The largest seed company in the world today is Shell Oil. Among the others are: Ciba-Geigy of Switzerland, Elf-Aquitaine of France, Hoechst of Germany, Occidental Petroleum of the U.S., and Cardo of Sweden.

We are concerned that most of these companies are also crop chemical manufacturers. With new developments in biotechnology, it is now less expensive to adapt the seed to the chemical than to design new chemicals for the seed. The thrust of corporate research is now on creating genetically uniform and patentable seeds that can be the conduit for one or more chemicals—and to engineer seeds that will tolerate spraying by otherwise toxic herbicides. In the North such trends mean increased costs, additional risks to the farmer and the environment and more chemical residues for the consumer. In the South—the largest and easiest market— increased risk means starvation. This year in Ethiopia one international chemical company came to the homeland of sorghum offering to sell a hybrid sorghum seed drawn from the seeds donated by Ethiopian farmers. This hybrid seed, which farmers could never save for another year, and which would create an annual dependence on the company for new seed, was to come coated in chemicals intended to make the seed amenable to the company's leading herbicides. This is not just. This is not Right Livelihood.

What has been given generously by the South is becoming private property in the North. It is unacceptable to argue that the work and human genius involved in developing new crop seeds in industrialized countries constitutes intellectual property, while the labor and genius of 500 generations of dedicated farmers in the Third World is either dumb luck or an act of God. This is not just. This must be changed.

We have been working on these problems with Third World countries for some time now. The Third World has developed its own solutions, however, in order to truly ensure that the first link in the food chain—the seeds and genes—are shared by all humanity. One of these solutions is to ask the governments of the world to place their gene banks under the auspices of the United Nations, thus ensuring that the seeds inside will be available to every nation regardless of their transient political differences. Spain and Costa Rica have already agreed to do this. We hope that the Nordic countries, who already have an international gene bank here in Sweden which they share together, could also place this gene bank under the flag of the United Nations.

Secondly, developing countries have also called for the creation of a multi-million dollar world gene fund, under United Nations control, which would allow for the conservation and development of the South's genetic heritage *in* the South. We hope that industrialized countries will see the justice and practicality of this proposal and support the fund.

From Nicaragua to Ethiopia to China there is recognition that a new and larger strategy is needed to secure our future food supply. We have learned four lessons over the years, and you will not be surprised to hear that the laws of nature and good science continue to go hand in hand with the laws of justice. One, we have learned that diversity can only be protected through a diversity of means and as Cary has already said, government gene banks must be regarded as a back-up to living collections and community seed banks. Two, we have learned that what is important to save depends on who we ask. Governments talk only to scientists about major crops. At the community level, genetic conservation means working with the women who garden and gather food, the herbalists who make medicines, the woodcutters and carpenters, the fisher folk and farmers, all of whom use plants, and value diversity. Three, we have learned that diversity must be used if it is to be prized and preserved, and that agricultural research today must redress the omissions of most of this century and work had in hand with farmers, in the laboratory offered by hundreds of thousands of fields and cultures. Four, we have learned that we cannot save the seed unless we also save the farmer, and the reverse is also true. The diversity of agriculture and human culture are bound together. In the end it is up to all of us, as governments and communities and individuals, to prize diversity. We must not shatter the first link in the food chain. The prayer, 'Give us this day our daily bread . . . ' must not become a prayer to Shell Oil or any country.

* *This speech was delivered jointly by Cary Fowler and Pat Mooney.*

WESTERN AFFLUENCE AND THIRD WORLD POVERTY

Leif Sandholt (on behalf of The Future in Our Hands)

9 December 1982

WHAT MAKES the thousands of Swedes, Danes, Finns and Norwegians in our movement accept a reduction in their economic standards of living? The reasons are many: we know that continued economic growth in our rich countries will be at the expense of those fellow human beings who really need an increase in material well-being—the under-privileged in the Third World.

We think it is senseless that eighty per cent of what is consumed in the world is consumed by the twenty per cent of humanity who live in the rich countries. We refuse to participate in continuing this unfairness between us and our brothers and sisters in the Third World.

So, first of all, our work is based on our human desire for justice. For many of us, this desire is also based on a feeling of moral and historical responsibility for the development which has led to today's lack of balance. One of the areas in the world most well-endowed by nature is Bengal, Bangladesh. Over two hundred years ago a development began which has made Bangladesh today one of the poorest nations in the world. From historical sources we know that, previously, this area was very rich with a flowering trade. There was an upper class living in great luxury—but in those days the majority also lived well!

The British entered Bengal in 1757 and began an almost

unrestricted exploitation, based on military power. New tax systems and property rights were introduced. Production of silk and muslin was interfered with in various ways, as England wanted to build up her own textile industry at home. The city of Dacca had 450,000 inhabitants in 1765, but thirty five years later the number had fallen to 20,000!

Can we imagine what changes in society must take place for a city to be reduced in thirty five years to 1/20th of its size?

Today Bangladesh has been independent for a decade but is totally dependent on the world market. The production of jute was inherited from colonial times. In 1974 jute represented eighty per cent of total export earnings. When the wheat harvest failed, the USA refused to sell wheat to Bangladesh until they stopped selling jute to Cuba, causing the death of several hundred thousand Bangladeshis.

In Sri Lanka the land used to provide plentiful food for the population. But then it was decided that the island should be the Western world's tea plantation, and it still is. In colonial times many such dependencies and trade structures were created. They still exist today, for as long as we in the rich countries want eighty per cent of what is produced on earth, we will not be prepared to let go of our political, economic and military domination of the Third World.

Much of today's development aid cements the impotence of the Third World. The World Bank decides agricultural policies and pushes the Green Revolution, which leads to a dependency on costly technology, pesticides and artificial fertilizers. This benefits only the rich and leaves more people without land. In Tanzania the World Bank demanded an end to free schooling and free health services, and to food and transport subsidies, as a pre-condition for a loan. We must get away from these unworthy dependency situations!

When we in the Future in Our Hands reduce our material living standards and create a 'new life-style', we see this as an act of solidarity, a way to level out the differences between the rich and the poor on earth. Of course a more just world does not follow automatically because someone chooses a new life-style. Even the Norwegian and Swedish authorities talk about 'moderation' today, but their motives are very different: they want us to compete better in the world market, to create the base for more economic growth.

So if we want our 'new life-style' to have a real effect, we must make sure that the surplus created is used to change society as a whole in the direction of more solidarity. But is it possible that a majority will agree to reduce their material standards? We think it is, because more and more people are finding that there is no connection between increased material living standards and happiness, contentment. As a wise man said 2000 years ago: 'What benefit is it to gain the whole world if the soul is damaged?"

During the last thirty years of increased living standards in Norway, suicides doubled, alcohol consumption doubled and drug use, including narcotics, also increased sharply. Violent crimes more than doubled and murders tripled. So it seems that the soul of our society has indeed been damaged, that we live in a less pleasant, less happy society today than twenty or thirty years ago.

In a 1975 opinion poll in Norway, two alternatives were presented: 'a pleasant and simple life with only necessities, with a limited income and limited career possibilities; or, high income, many material goods and career possibilities but with possible stress at work and off work'. Seventy five per cent of those questioned chose the first alternative. When asked if they believed that an increased income would mean a richer life or more problems, three out of four replied that to them this would mean more problems or no improvement.

We want to participate in creating a just sharing of the world's resources—for those who live today and for future generations. This means that we must reduce our consumption of resources, and see that the surplus is transferred to the poor in the Third World in a way which benefits their own development and does not create a new dependence. The surplus should also be used to change our society, so that it as a whole becomes more co-operative. Our aim of getting away from considering the material profitability of everything we do, will benefit our own countries also. It will open possibilities for human contact and co-operation which today are sacrificed in the race for 'effectiveness'.

We believe that active human solidarity should be the criteria for valuing our acts, thoughts and deeds. We believe that everyone has the right to social and material conditions which enable them to develop their potential, as far as possible without preventing others from exercising this right now or in the future. We believe that we must preserve our biological life environment, if our quality of life is to be preserved. All who act according to these values may use the name Future in Our Hands. We ask all to think for themselves and to find their own solutions based on these values. As a result, many individuals, groups and organisations used our name or count themselves as part of our movement.

We think it is important for each one of us to decide if we want to be part of the world's problems or part of the solution: at the moment when we begin to evaluate our actions and make our choices from the point of view of all of us in the world, instead of from individual or national viewpoints, a basic and great change takes place.

We believe that we as humans and fellow humans together can take the future in our hands.

CHAPTER THREE

The Cooperative Community

The Cooperative Community

THE MOST extreme experiences of poverty and exploitaiton occur in the countries of the Third World, and the burdens of poverty fall most heavily on the shoulders of the women. The story of the hardships faced by the women of Ahmedabad in the north west of India is told by Ela Bhatt, in her speech on behalf of the Self-Employed Women's Association (SEWA-meaning service). The SEWA story is not one of subjection to exploitation, but of an inspirational initiative which has succeeded in forging, against huge odds, an organisation which has combined in a dynamic fashion the functions of trades unionism and co-operation. SEWA's existence dates back to 1971 when a group of women, working as cart pullers in Ahmedabad's market, approached the Textile Labour Association for help. At the time Ela Bhatt was head of the women's wing of the union. The outcome of the meeting was the formation of SEWA, which went on to assist in the formation of similar and related organisations in eight other Indian states. SEWA has organised self-employed women who have consequently been better able to protect themselves from the male money lenders and merchants who have determined their working conditions. SEWA has united a variety of women in different trades, many of them separated by caste and religion. Although it varies from trade to trade, up to 40% of the women are the sole supporters of their families, the men having deserted or migrated for work elsewhere. On top of its trade union function, SEWA has set up its own bank with 23,000 members, and it has developed cooperative wholesale and marketing support to enable the women to get better rewards for their work. The SEWA initiative is an inspirational one, providing a practical and symbolic example of the power of co-operative organisation to transcend the fragmentation and severe exploitation characteristic of economic relationships throughout the Third World.

The Participarory Institute for Development Alternatives (PIDA) was formed in 1980 to promote grass roots participatory initiatives in Sri Lanka. It is an action-research collective with a core membership of fifteen 'animators', who work in ten rural and one urban location, in order to stimulate the communities to develop self-reliant economic initiatives. Sri Lankan village society suffers from divisions common throughout the Asian world. In particular there is a division between the majority of small producers (whether farmers, artisans, fishermen or wage-earners), and a minority of merchants, traders, moneylenders, large landowners, and bureaucrats. The relationship between the two groups is an unequal one, and a sequence of causes (low prices for products, high rents, low wages, exhorbitant interest charges, corruption, etc.), results in impoverishment, and in attitudes and values which support a debilitating dependency. The approach which PIDA takes in its attempt to break this dependency is comprehensively described in the speech of S. Tilakaratna on behalf of PIDA. "While PIDA aims to build self-reliance, the work of Anwar Fazal is aimed at removing the damage caused to those who have been tempted away from self-reliance into the global supermarket and subjected to a trade which . . . is more like an armed attack" (1)

Anwar Fazal has been involved with the consumer protection movement since 1968. He is a founder of the Consumers Association of Penang, and has been a consultant on consumer affairs for the Government of Mauritius and the Hong Kong Consumer Council. During 1977, while acting as a consultant for the United Nations Food and Agricultural Organisation, he drafted a 'Code of Ethics for the International Trade in Food'. He is the president of the International Organisation of Consumers Unions (IOCU) which coordinates the work of consumer organisations in fifty countries. Since 1978, Fazal has been concerned to organise the consumer movement, through the IOCU, against the abuses of multinational corporations, who have often been the main culprits in the dumping of hazardous products, especially in Third World markets. In addition to his work as President of the IOCU, and in the Consumers Association of Penang, Fazal has been prominent in the work of four significant global consumers networks. Consumer Interpol is an alert system monitoring hazardous products, processes and wastes. The International Baby Food Action Network (IBFAN), is a coalition of groups concerned about the trade in infant feeding powders, and about the discouragement, for commercial reasons, of breast feeding. The Pesticides Action Network unites groups working on the nature of pesticides used in agriculture, while Health Action International (HAI) monitors the use and advertising of pharmaceutical products. Two thirds of the membership of IOCU comes from Third World countries.

Fazal recognises that his work is not merely a matter of consumer protection in the narrow sense; it is not a case of helping aggrieved consumers to get value for money. In a very direct sense he argues that wasteful consumption is destroying society and doing violence to individuals and communities. The Pesticides Action Network (PAN), for example, was formed in 1982 with the support of the IOCU and Friends of the Earth, Malaysia, and actively campaigns to put an end to pesticide abuse. Fazal has argued that hundreds of thousands of people in the Third World are being poisoned because of the irresponsible marketing practices of multinational agrochemical corporations. In response to the recognition of a growing range of abuses, people are becoming aware of the power which they hold through co-operation as consumers. They can use this power against larger power-structures in society, particularly against the combined abuses of governments and business corporations. The cooperative consumers movement is a growing one. The principles and concerns which guide its activities are concisely outlined in Anwar Fazal's speech.

PLENTY USA emerged from an initiative taken in the early 1970s. It was inspired originally by the experiences and values of the hippie culture, and is described in more detail in this section in the speech of Stephen Gaskin. It was born from the realisation that all people share a common heritage, and that if the abundance of the earth is used wisely, there is plenty for all. Since it was founded in 1974, Plenty volunteers have worked in twelve countries and four continents. Its projects are designed to enhance self-sufficiency, self-determination, and well-being, and are practical responses to poverty and injustice. In particular, Plenty feels a close affinity with native Indian cultures around the world: "We believe it to be essential that native societies, with their ancient traditions of reverence for life and the earth, should not be swept aside in an unthinking rush for 'progress' and profit." (2)

Plenty began its work with the distribution of food surpluses from its Tennessee farm to deprived communities, initially in rural Tennessee, then to groups in urban Nashville, Memphis, Chicago, and Detroit. By 1975-76 the organisation had extended its assistance to victims of natural disasters in Honduras, Haiti, and Guatemala. It was in Guatemala, following the earthquake of 1976, that Plenty came to know of the problems of the Mayan Indians, and stayed on to work with them until "Civil war and a worsening campaign of indiscriminate violence waged against the highland Mayans forced us to withdraw our volunteers from Guatemala in 1980." (3)

The experience in Guatemala introduced Plenty to the realities of life in the Third World, and to the problems faced by native cultures.

"The Guatemalan Indian has few options in hard times. He is rooted in the ancient Mayan traditions of family, tribe, and community cooperation, but caught between the excessive ideologies of the superpowers; forced, at gunpoint, to take sides in a politically polarised situation that leaves no middle ground . . . the rural Indians want neither repression nor revolution. Certainly they'd like some things to change, but they have a deep and abiding commitment to peace. They are a people who are known for their humble ways, their firmly rooted spirituality, their frugal but joyful lifestyle, their amazing strength and perseverance. That they are systematically being destroyed is one of the greatest unspoken tragedies of our time." (4)

"Stephen Gaskin founded the farm Community ten years ago as a means of preserving and putting into daily practice the idealism of the hippie movement: nonviolence, hospitality, sharing. The farm is an example of that spiritual revolution today which—far from implying a withdrawal from worldly activity—works to save and change the planet by showing in practise that love and sharing, not greed and envy, are the characteristics most in tune with our inner selves." (5)

In the spirit of its original foundation, Plenty works on a wide range of initiatives. Since 1979 it has worked on low cost housing schemes in the South Bronx, New York, where it also runs a community medical service. In Lesotho it has promoted integrated village development with projects in reforestation, solar energy, and rural health centres. It has developed soyfood cooperatives in the Caribbean; free midwifery and primary health care clinics; and self-sufficiency projects among native American communities. In the wide range of its practical work for right livelihood and cooperation, it was an appropriate winner of the first award of the Foundation in 1980.

1. Jakob von Uexkull, Introductory Speech, 1982
2. Plenty brochure, 1985
3. Plenty brochure, 1985
4. Statement of the Plenty Refugee Fund.
5. Jakob von Uexkull, Indroductory Speech, 1985

RURAL DEVELOPMENT

S. Tilakaratna (on behalf of PIDA)

9th December 1982

THE Participarory Institute for Development Alternatives (PIDA) is not an isolated initiative in an isolated island. We are a part of a wider process towards 'another development' in the Asian context. We have built up useful linkages with grass root movements and groups in different parts of Asia, and continuous interaction is taking place among these groups, enriching each other's experiences and initiatives.

Although PIDA is still a young organisation, no more than two years old as an independent entity, our roots go back to the mid-seventies when a team of Asian scholars, centered around the UN Asian Institute of Development in Bangkok, initiated a process of reflection on the reality of Asian poverty, the failure of past developmental efforts, and attempted to develop a conceptual framework for an alternative development in Asia.

Asia is predominantly a rural society. For about three decades, Asian countries have adopted an imitative and an alien development model with industrialisation, growth of the modern sector, transfer of capital and technology, 'trickle down' and some kind of 'top-down' planning as the central elements. In many countries the model failed on its own terms. Moreover, what resulted was maldevelopment; the society was polarised and people were alienated from their culture and tradition. Relentless forces that produce poverty continued unabated. Poverty has in fact increased, both under conditions of stagnancy in production, and in situations of greatly increased production.

The conventional model failed and became less and less accepted. It was in this context that the team of Asian scholars began their search for alternatives. They studied the macro as well as micro development processes going on in Asian countries and evolved a conceptual framework, 'Toward a Theory of Rural Development'. The internal dynamics of an Asian grass roots movement (Bhoomisena in India) was studied in depth, using participatory research methodology which helped to sharpen further the conceptualisation on alternative development. People's knowledge and practice at the grass roots interacted with modern knowledge and scientific analysis, to produce a new praxis on how the creative initiatives of the people of rural Asia may be released and mobilized for all round development of their livelihood.

The next logical step was to undertake an experimental project to translate the theory into operational terms and to train a group of personnel in participatory action research. Sri Lanka was selected for this experimentation, and an action research project was started under the auspices of the government and with UN resource support. The project trained a core group of action researchers over a period of some eighteen months, who in turn trained village level cadres ('change agents') for initiating the new praxis of people's development at the village level. The project proved a success. PIDA was born out of this experiment. It was set up in August 1980 by a group of action researchers trained under this project and assisted by the scholars who pioneered the search for an alternative development in Asia.

PIDA's Vision of Development.

We look at development in fundamental humanistic terms,

as a process of overall development of the people and their potential. Bringing out the creativity and the potential of the people is the means as well as the end of development. People are the subjects and not mere objects or targets of development. There are several important aspects to such a humanistic view of development:

- Development cannot be delivered to the people as a package from outside. It is essentially an endogenous process which stems from the heart of each society.
- Development can acquire its full meaning only if rooted at the local level and in the praxis of each primary community. Development is first and foremost lived by the people where they are, where they work and live, that is in the first instance at the local level.
- No development model can be universal. In fact the richness of development consists in its variety and plurality of patterns deeply ingrained in the culture and tradition of each society. Attempts at uniformity and universalism are mechanistic, and alienates people.
- Self reliance, participation and countervailing power are central components in the development process as conceived by us. The three concepts are a unity, an integrated whole. Self-reliance is not to be confused with the narrow concepts of autarchy and self-sufficiency. It is rather an autonomous capacity to take decisions affecting one's livelihood, and to choose one's course of development uninhibited by external influences. It is a reappropriation of man's control over his livelihood and environment, hitherto alienated to others. It is a process of self-assertion. It aims at breaking away from dominant-dependent relationships, and forging relationships on an equal footing. Participation as a central democratic value is organically linked with the assertion of self-reliance, for it denotes that people acting through their own free-will

take decisions pertaining to their lives. Participation requires organised efforts to increase control over resources and institutions on the part of the people who have hitherto been excluded from such control. Liberation from domination and exploitation requires that people build up and exercise a measure of counterpower to the dominant interests in the society. Power dominates. Countervailing power liberates.

PIDA works primarily with the rural poor in Sri Lanka. An important point of departure for PIDA's work is that rural communities are not homogeneous entities. The existence of conflicting (rather than harmonious) interests is a fundamental fact of village life. In general, the basic social structure in a village is characterised by the existence of a dominant interest (such as traders-cum-money lenders, landowners, rural elite and even rural bureaucrats) who benefit from the status quo, and the minority, consisting of the small and marginal farmers, other peasants, landless workers, and rural artisans who live in poverty. In this context, most rural institutions, and so called 'neutral' interventions in rural areas by governments as well as voluntary agencies, get adjusted to the dynamics of these contraditions and end up by benefitting the dominant interests, and perpetuating the status quo.

While there is a conflict of interest between different classes and groups in the rural society, they are also mutually dependent on one another. These relationships are, however, asymmetrical in form, and assume a dominant-dependent character, an unequal dependency relationship. The small commodity producers (whether small farmer or rural artisan), for example, lose a considerable portion of their incomes (economic surplus) to money lenders, traders, landowners and the bureaucrats. Exorbitant interest rates; low product prices and high input prices (lower terms of trade); high land rents; and corruption work against them.

The drain of economic surplus through dependency links (dominant/dependent relationships) creates a process of impoverishment, suppresses the rural productive forces, and keeps the productivity of the rural economy at a low level of equilibrium.

These asymmetrical relationships also create dependency attitudes among the rural poor; mental attitudes and value systems are created to legitimise the dependency relationships, and the existing social structures. More over, the poor themselves are not a homogeneous category, being divided by caste and many other issues. They also compete with each other for the limited economic opportunities in the village. These factors, namely dependency attitudes and disunity, inhibit the poor from taking initiatives to improve their lot, and tend to make them non-innovative, non-problem solving, non-experimental, and acquiescent with the status quo. This in turn reinforces and stabilises the asymmetrical dependency relationships, and a vicious circle of dependency and poverty is created.

This explains why it is difficult, if not impossible, for a self-reliant rural development process to be a spontaneously generated process. A catalytic intervention is, more often than not, a necessary initial input in the mobilisation as well as conscientisation of the rural poor for organised action to achieve self-reliant development.

Issues for the future.

Our experience is that there is always some political and economic space to initiate a process of self-reliant development at the grass roots (village) level. Moreover, such space does not remain static but expands with each successful action. For one thing, people's confidence in their ability to change the reality is enhanced. For another, improvement in the economic status of the people, and the creation of group funds, enhances the capacity to undertake further actions. When a number of peoples' groups emerge in a locality, and the isolation is broken down, inter-group interaction takes place and linkages are forged among groups, providing a future source of encouragement and strength. PIDA's experience in working with a variety of groups reveal that a process of mobilisation, conscientisation, and organisation can be initiated under different economic and social conditions and the development process is replicable. These are very interesting and useful results in themselves; peoples' initiatives have been liberated (within limits of course), and a degree of countervailing power to local power structures has been built up.

What are the prospects of such grass root initiatives expanding beyond the local level to become a countervailing power at the national level? How far are grass root micro processes capable of ultimately expanding into national macro level movements? How far do grass root initiatives represent the first glimpses of a new liberated society? These questions take us to an area where a single organisation such as PIDA acting alone can do little. There is a need to build a network of linkages within a country, among grass root organisations as well as with 'friendly' organisations, institutions, and groups, so that a protective cover is available for a wider movement arising from grass roots initiatives.

Grass root initiatives are still a very controversial animal in many Third World countries. Often they have been looked upon with suspicion, and sometimes they have been interpreted as 'subversive' moves of some kind. They often run the risk of either co-option or repression. Hence grass root initiatives need legitimacy and recognition if they are to move away from the marginal place, which they currently occupy, to the main stream of social life. They have to be recognised as effective methods of reaching the poor, and of fostering participation, which is a basic human right. A government committed to another development, and to participation as a basic human right, could go a long way in creating the necessary political climate for grass root initiatives to expand into wider social movements. But such political environments are getting increasingly scarce in the Third World. One encouraging feature is that many inter-governmental organisations, in particular some parts of the UN system, have shown an increasing interest in introducing community participation as an important component into their Third World development projects. PIDA itself has assisted several UN agencies in this regard. The enlightened sections of the international community can play an important role by acting as a lobby/pressure group to facilitate more space, legitimacy and protection to grass root initiatives operating 'another development'.

WOMEN'S DEVELOPMENT IN INDIA

Ela Bhatt, (on behalf of SEWA)

9th December 1984

ON BEHALF of my sisters in SEWA, I am here to express our deep sense of gratitude for the honour bestowed on us by conferring the Right Livelihood Award. The Award has reassured us that we are on the right track in our endeavour. It is a recognition not only of SEWA, but also an honour to the non-industrial world, to the self employed workers of the world, who are not destined to live depressed for ever. Let me introduce the women of SEWA to you, their struggles, achievements and hopes.

Maku is a vegetable vendor who borrows $5 from a private moneylender early in the morning, and repays $5.5 in the evening from her tiny income. This would go on day after day, all her life. But Maku, along with Laxmi, Raji, Mangu and others got organised and created a Cooperative Bank of their own. The authorities said, how can you ever have banking with illiterate and poor women? But the women did manage to establish their own bank in 1974, and thus shattered the myth that poor, illiterate women cannot run a Bank. They have run it profitably for a decade. Today about 20,000 such Makus and Laxmis have their savings accounts in the Bank and take loans to recover their mortgaged land, house and silver, and possess production tools of their own. They elect the Director Board, (each member representing a trade), which manages the working capital of 800,000 dollars.

The repayment rate of loans is 98%. SEWA Bank is now on the list of the Reserve (Federal) Bank of India, and affiliated with Women's World Banking, New York.

Let me introduce other sisters of SEWA. Here is Jashoda. She sells fish in the downtown market called Manekchowk. She refuses to please the policemen on the beat, so she is in trouble. Then there is Suraj, who sells fruit in the market. She was even born in the Manekchowk market. There are 500 such vendors in the market. In January 1980, the city authorities decided to solve the traffic problem in the market by removing all vendors. The vendors got organised in SEWA, and went to complain before the Police Commissioner and Municipal Commissioner, but the appeal proved futile. So the vendor sisters organised a 'Satyagraha', and stood alongside their vegetable baskets in peaceful defiance of the police orders. Gandhian thinking is our source of inspiration. In January 1980 the defensive action won back their old place. But this was no permanent solution. So, in 1982, the vendors and SEWA filed a Petition in the Supreme Court of India seeking the right to do business, i.e. to have official licenses. In 1984, by Court Order, they got the vending licenses in Manekchowk Market, where they have been vending for three or four generations. This was a turning point in the present urban policy.

A large number of the working population in every city or town consists of hawkers and vendors, slumdwellers and pavement dwellers. Are they not an integral part of our city population? They provide an essential distribution service to the community, and to industries. They create their own employment, making no demands on the society. But they have no place in the city planning. As the city expands they are arbitrarily removed and made workless, homeless. Often they are treated like antisocials! Negative attitudes are deeply entrenched. The middle class citizens look down upon them as dirty, loud. The authorities and planners see them as a nuisance and a traffic obstruction. This is a common problem in most of the cities of the developing countries. Our planners want their cities like those of the West. We need our own cities. We need to respect our own people, their work, their life-styles and traditions, and observe the incessant flow and exchange between villages and urban centres—the emergence of 'new cities'—rural cities I would call them. Do cities always have to be urban?

Let me introduce Radha, 45 years old, a headloader in the Cloth Market. She goes to work at 8am and waits for work. She carries headloads from shop to shop and gets paid per trip. She earns two dollars at the end of the day. Before she was organised in 1979, she earned only half a dollar. Surely Radha works as hard as any factory worker, or as hard as any office employee. Surely her work is as essential as theirs? But where are the trade unions who will defend Radha's right to work, to job security, to a living wage? Baluben is a weaver in the village. She weaves woollen blankets and is paid at piecerate. The rate is very low. She can be fired from work any time. She is too weak to raise her demand. Balamma coughs all day, spits blood because she is a cigarette roller. She is at the mercy of the contractor in spite of having laws protecting her wages. Babuben picks up rags and wastepaper from the street, sells the haul to a wastepaper merchant. Jivatba is a fuelwood picker in the mountains. She collects fuel for the whole day, sells the headload for one and a half dollars, which literally earns her daily bread. Often she gets beaten up by people from the Forest Department. During the cotton season, thousands of women unshell cottonpods, and get paid at piece rate. Where are the trade unions to protect their rights? When are the problems of the self-employed going to be discussed in the halls of the International Labour Organisation? Kanku, Lali, and Chandra are all agriculture workers. They have employment for hardly five months of a year. Their struggle for higher wages failed for lack of bargaining power. They changed their strategy. They learnt new skills, revived the traditional ones and formed dairy, weavers, and labour supply cooperatives. Kanku, a landless labourer says, 'I have a handloom, and a buffalo and a calf—and now I am able to bargain for higher agriculture wages from the landlord'!

The bamboo workers survive on bamboocraft, but bamboo is getting more and more expensive. The bamboo they buy at 2 dollars per piece is sold at half a pence to the Paper Factory! How can they defend themselves against the onslaught of big industries?

There is a limit to the effect of trade union struggles, in the absence of legal support. Hence, SEWA had to evolve alternative economic bodies, primarily co-ops. The handblock printers being displaced by screenprinters upgraded their skills, learnt accountancy and management, formed their own co-op. The bamboo workers followed suit. Waste paper pickers plan a village-level paper factory. Woodcutters are being absorbed by the Forest Department in plantation. Two woodcutter women have been appointed as Forest Guards!

Technology? Yes, we welcome technology which improves our living and working conditions, but we do not want technology that snatches away whatever little work we have. We are rural women, spending half our life fetching home water, fuel and fodder. We want them at our doorstep. We are artisans, help us to create better tools for faster production. Take us to an expanded market, but that which is within our reach. Help us to improve our brooms, baskets and pushcarts. We face occupational hazards. We unshell peanuts with our teeth (the nation earns foreign exchange out of them), but our lips and mouth get so sore that we cannot eat food. When we unshell cottonpods our fingers bleed. We break stones, we breathe stone dust, we sweep the streets, we load and load cement bags and fill our lungs with dust and cement, we roll cigarettes and breathe tobacco. We pull carts of 2000 kgs, and lose our unborn babes. We are not ready to accept this life for our daughters. Renowned researchers have made miracles—

like transplanting hearts or reaching the moon. Will our Research Institutes hurry up to design a proper mask, a glove, a footstool, a hammer, a fingercap for our workers?

Most often human capacities are underestimated by us, hence we put blind faith in machines, which leads to centralisation of money and power. Even the present structures—legal, economic and social, including trade unions and cooperatives, fail to cater to the need of our people. For whom do we build our towns, roads, industries, markets, schools and laboratories? Let us ask ourselves. Is it really the few big dams, or the huge industrial plants or metropolis, that change the face of the world? Even a small uplift of the capacities of the people is able to bring total change in the world.

Without any model or a blueprint to follow, SEWA started its work in 1972. The SEWA women, by organising themselves, have faced many struggles, gulped bitterness, but in the process have attained self dignity, a slice of power, They have increased their ability to think, act, react, manage and lead. From a miserable passive acceptance of all the injustices, they have attained courage to stand up and fight. Self-reliance is what they want ultimately. There is no development without self-reliance. But there is no shortcut to self-reliance, except by organisation.

SEWA is struggling to find alternatives in a society based on love and non violence, to develop forums for the privileged and unprivileged to hold hands without exploitation.

This is an uphill fight, an arduous economic war. My colleagues and myself are like matchsticks which are used to light lamps. Matchsticks are useless once their task is over, but they do dispel some darkness in the darkest corners. To kindle our innumerable lamps, the Right Livelihood Award is a Magnificent Matchstick, for which I again thank the Foundation on behalf of SEWA.

INTERNATIONAL AID

Stephen Gaskin, (on behalf of PLENTY)

9th December 1980

THE FARM was started as a way to be independent and to follow our ideals. Our intention was to do something creative about how to live. We left San Fransisco on October 10th 1970, and we travelled: twenty five or thirty buses with 250 hippies. Those people had come from all over the U.S. and all over the world in the sixties to San Fransisco, to follow the call that came from there, that there was something new happening about spirit and relationships and human-kind.

I was a little older. I was over 30 before they said 'don't trust anyone over 30'. I'd already been to Korea, and to combat, and to college. I had a master's degree, and had taught in college for a couple of years. So I had some other experiences. We travelled on the road in that great caravan for seven months, 250 to 400 people. Travelling around the U.S., I was talking in schools and churches. This was the time when the demonstrating students were shot by the National Guard at Kent State University. The youth of America were trembling on the brink of violence. I went around the country and said that we can't get violent, it will dishonour what we're doing if we become violent.

We became a community on the road. We had to give things up and learn new things. Some of us had to give up welfare. I knew they would take the caravan off the road if they thought it was running on welfare. I knew we wouldn't survive if any of us were dope dealers. We had to give these things up to be together. Being together was the most valuable thing we found. When we got back to San Fransisco we couldn't exist as a caravan in the city, they wouldn't allow it. We couldn't park in Golden Gate Park, with 250 hippies, and start cultivating the land.

On our travels we had met some nice farmers in Tennessee, so we went back there. We found a farm and we moved on to it. The first piece of land we bought was 1,000 acres for $70 an acre. We now have 1,750 acres of rolling hills. That is about five or six square kilometres. Of the original 250 people who came we still have 150 with us, because we have a high commitment. We now have 1,600 people living on that farm. We have other farms and centres in New York, California, and elsewhere. We have an ambulance service in the South Bronx in New York, one of the most bombed-out looking places in the world.

When we went to the land we were like a beach head, like going up on the beach and digging a hole in the sand and trying to survive. We'd had to give up a certain amount of ego, like demanding a large living space, having a car for each one of us. It was good for us, but after about four years we saw that we would become stagnant if we didn't reach out beyond us. So we formed PLENTY INTERNATIONAL. There is *plenty* if it were accurately distributed. We really believe that. Our ideal was based on the idea that if you had a random selection of people in the world and they all went collective with what they had, the strength that they would have collectively would make all of them viable, all of them able to make it. We still believe that.

In the meantime other things were happening. Don Etkins, a white South African who had to leave his country to avoid being drafted to fight in Angola, worked on our project for one and a half years, then on the farm for another one and a half years. By this time he was a well trained international volunteer. He said he wanted to take PLENTY to Africa, so he went to Lesotho. We have been given a nice piece of land, near a river, to grow food to support our volunteers, and to build an experimental village incorporating our ideas, introducing the soy bean, and trying to stop the erosion of land which is not being farmed because the men are off mining gold.

Then somebody from the U.N. said 'I'll tell you a place that really needs help. The U.N. can't do anything about it because the U.S.A. is too rich, but the Bronx in New York City needs help badly.' We went to the South Bronx. You would not believe it. It looks like Dresden after the fire bombing. Miles of flat rubble. You know who did that? Young black children and insurance companies and landlords. The black children out of revolution, and the insurance companies and landlords out of greed. We moved in there. One of the things we had learnt was to take care of ourselves medically. In the U.S. it costs 2,000 dollars to have a baby. So we could not afford retail medical care. In Tennessee the state gave free lessons on how to be an emergency medical technician. This means that you can give heart massage, mouth to mouth resuscitation, drive the ambulance, etc. We took the courses until we reached the level where we could teach them to others.

We went to the South Bronx with a second-hand ambulance and set up an ambulance service. We started courses with the local folk so that they could learn the techniques of reviving people etc. and maintaining the ambulance. The city ambulances took forty five minutes or one hour to get there, and a lot of people died. We came in seven minutes. The police don't carry the city hospital number in the South Bronx. They call us. Down in Alabama the police cars used to carry bumper stickers saying 'You don't like cops? Next time you need help call a hippie.' We have a bumper sticker now saying 'Next time you want help call a hippie: PLENTY'. We have redeemed the hippie ideal. It was not a fad. It was a style or fashion, it was a change of life.

At the farm we live on 700 dollars per person per year. That is 300 dollars less than the Navajo Indians live on. We operate on one seventh of the level of money that it would take to be taxable. We are well below the official U.S. poverty level. But we are not poor. We are strong, because our collectivity has made us that way. As Hassan Fathy said, when a man helps another to build a house he knows that part of his pay is that the other man will come back and help him build his house. This is the basis of everything we do. We have learnt to deliver babies the same way. We delivered over 1,300 children, only about half of them ours. The others came from all over the world to the Farm to have their baby. People will travel thousands of miles to go to a farm that has dirt roads, and live poverty style with a bunch of hippies, rather than go to a brand new shiny hospital to have their baby! We have now developed a large enough statistic to show that our deliveries are safer, for both mothers and children, than in the U.S. and many other countries. We have been following the natural process. Our midwives made the assumption that if the process wasn't pretty perfect, how did we get here? There have only been doctors for seventy five years. The natural process is perfect by itself about 98% of the time, we find. The midwife recognises the other 2% early and consults a specialist then.

When we started deliveries we felt that having a baby was a sacrament. In the old days the sacraments belonged to the family. Dying is also a sacrament. In my opinion, the preoccupation with violence in the entertainment media is because people are insulated from real life. You don't see a death unless you have a white uniform. If you are not a doctor and have been through twelve years of college you are not privileged to see a death. The people who can't see real death watch it on T.V. We've made it into a mystery and put it behind closed doors.

We happen just by accident to be a very well educated group. We have more degrees on the Farm than the state legislature has. We have the number you'd expect in a small college. So we have strong opinions about nuclear power, because we understand it pretty good. Some of our technicians invented this little machine which we call the Nuke Buster. It has elements of a geiger counter and a foetal heart monitor. It detects and measures background radiation. It can count from normal background, but we don't really know what that is anymore since Madame Curie, because all the uranium was dug up and is now on the surface of the earth, which God has very wisely stashed below the surface so that it didn't bother anybody. We have taken it out and reduced it to its most poisonous form and turned it loose. We make this instrument on the Farm. It is one of the cottage industries that we survive by.

I'm in this battle about the nukes because I know we are being lied to. Here is a gasolene lantern with its silk bag. Watch this! (The nuke buster registers a very high count) Ain't that something? There is no label on it to say it is radioactive. You can buy it anywhere. We found it was radioactive by accident. There are hundreds of consumer products on the market that are radioactive. Appropriate technology is that which is good for the people, and does not destroy the rest of the culture. This instrument we feel is important because without something to see those rays with, they are like magic. This is a magical instrument.

THE CONSUMER MOVEMENT

Anwar Fazal

9th December 1982

ONE DAY some three years ago in the village of Banjaran in Indonesia, the silence was broken by beating drums, bringing together some 200 people.

The people marched to a nearby chemical factory and burned it to the ground. The factory had poisoned their water. It had destroyed their once productive field and ignored orders by local officials to curb the flow of toxic waste. The factory had failed to deliver a promised US $1,800 compensation to the affected farmers.

The villagers had for years been trying to get the factory to improve its waste disposal practices. The drums of the village of Banjaran are now silent and the farmers had to pay the price of taking the law into their own hands—they had to go to prison. Waters poisoned, rice fields rendered infertile, factories burned, lives destroyed, and people crushed. This is the kind of tragic world we live in, a world in which 50,000 people die each day from lack of clean water and sanitation while each minute the world spends US$1 million on weapons. We live in a world in which violence, waste and manipulation have not only become central elements in our lives but which have become profitable for the merchants of death, the rapists of the earth, and those who manipulate our behaviour, our fears and desires.

VIOLENCE — it has been estimated that

pharmaceutical companies may be responsible for a minimum of ten to fifteen million cases of injury and one million deaths each year among the three billion people in the developing world. Conservative figures suggest that at least 375,000 people in the Third World are poisoned yearly by pesticides and, of them, at least 10,000 die because of pesticides that are very often not permitted in the countries of origin.

WASTE—no figures can sufficiently describe the wanton destruction and misuse of resources, of processes, and of products in our society. We see the destruction of the tropical forests, and the waste of meagre incomes by poor people in the Third World on useless, inappropriate products—products they do not need nor can afford. In Bangladesh, it was once said that the bulk of the vitamins bought were purchased by people who did not need them and they mostly were excreted as urine—vitamised urine is a luxury that Bangladesh can do without!

MANIPULATION—Probably one of the greatest behavioural changes occurred in the way in which the natural self reliant method of feeding babies with milk from the mothers breast was subverted and supplemented by two kinds of so called 'modern technologies'—the technology of processed cows milk and the technology of marketing. We see pervasive manipulation of people's behaviour through advertising and promotional tactics that border, in certain industries, on the criminal and immoral—offering a variety of bribes. This subversion of breast feeding itself has been associated with health problems among ten million infants a year. James Grant, Director of UNICEF, has said that if we can protect and promote breast feeding we can save the lives of one million infants a year.

What can be done about this violence, this waste, this manipulation? I would like to share with you what organised consumers in the 'consumer movement' can do about such issues.

The consumer movement is about five important things:

First, the consumer movement is about people—people who care about society from a very special perspective, a perspective which concerns every single human being, man, woman and child. This perspective is about ourselves as consumers of goods and services, produced and provided both by commercial and government sectors. It is about the availability of these goods and services. It is not just about the cost of living but more often the cost of survival! It is not just about value for money, but more about value for people.

Secondly, the consumer is about power—the power of ordinary people to organise themselves collectively, to serve as a countervailing force to promote and protect their interests as consumers. It involves also power to act jointly against those responsible for the violent, wasteful and manipulative actions against us; and power to change the structures that permit this violence, this waste and this manipulation.

Thirdly, the consumer movement is about human rights—the right to a decent life with dignity, the right to organise ourselves to protect our interest. In particular it is about seven consumer rights: the right to have our basic needs to survive met efficiently and equitably; our right to safety; our right to redress and compensation; our right to representation; our right to adequate information; our right to consumer education, and our right to a healthy environment.

Fourthly, the consumer movement is also about the environment—about a sustainable earth. We must not only be concerned with serving and protecting the insides of our bodies, our 'inner limits' but also be concerned with the 'outer limits' of mother earth—a powerful, complex and yet fragile and exploitable structure. This structure gives us the opportunity for a good life, but it can also be destroyed, not by people's needs but by people's greed, ignorance and carelessness. Consumers must be conservers also.

Fifthly, the consumer movement is about justice, about the way in which political, legal and economic systems are organised to bring about a just, fair and rational basis for living together.

These five pillars are the basis on which to judge the relevance, the competence and the success of the consumer movement. They are very much an integral part of the work of the International Organization of Consumers Unions (IOCU)—work that has caused us at the global level to deal with the power of the transnational corporations; with the possibilities that lie with international institutions; and with the development of global citizens' networks.

We have been involved in the baby milk issue, with issues relating to the pharmaceutical companies, and with pesticides. In order to deal with the issue of the dumping of banned and restricted products we have initiated a global citizens' network called the 'Consumer Interpol'. This network is a rapid information exchange and investigative system among citizens groups about such products, and coordinates global action around the issue of dumping.

IOCU now links the work of over one hundred and twenty consumer groups in some fifty countries, at every stage of development, and in every continent. Through the new networks of citizens' groups we have helped to create the International Baby Food Action Group (IBFAN)—the Health Action International (HAI) and the Pesticides Action Network (PAN). We are associated with hundreds of consumer, community action, development, environment, women's and trade union groups which take our work to millions of ordinary people—(from mothers who boycott Nestle products because of the way the company has been marketing cows milk to babies; to doctors, who boycott Ciba Geigy products because of its association with one of the worst drug disasters of all times, caused by the drug clioquinol).

The work of consumer groups has had a great impact. There is now an international code for promoting and protecting breastfeeding. Ciba Geigy have recently announced they will withdraw oral preparations of the drug clioquinol all over the world. We hope through the work of 'Consumer Interpol' and the other citizens' networks to reduce, if not eliminate, the violence, the waste and the manipulation that characterises so much of our society. We shall do this in ways that are as humane as our ends.

CHAPTER FOUR

Human Centered Technology

Human Centered Technology

THE VALUES which are applied to the design and use of technology form a central concern of right livelihood. The most harmonious and integrated systems of human social organisation, and the intricate interconnectedness of the natural world, can be torn apart by the vast array of technologies deployed by the force of industrialism. Lewis Mumford made a distinction between authoritarian and democratic technics, between technologies which enslave and technologies which liberate. Schumacher popularised the idea that human happiness depended on the development, not of mass technology, but of a technology of the masses, a people's technology. Amongst the most exciting recent attempts to provide both substance and practical application to the notion of a democratic or people's technology was the initiative of the Lucas Aerospace Combine Shop Stewards Committee represented here by the speech of Mike Cooley. Significantly, the Lucas initiative attempted to raise the possibility of designing and applying what they called socially useful technologies, not as a marginal activity, but from *within* one of the largest multinational corporations operating in the world. Significantly also, the company is one of the most prominent manufacturers of sophisticated weapons technologies and components.

Lucas Aerospace is part of Lucas Industries and was by the early 1970s the largest single manufacturer of aircraft systems and equipment in the United Kingdom. About 50% of its work was directly concerned with the manufacture of military aircraft. The Lucas Combine Committee was formed in 1969, to unite and represent the various groups of rank and file workers from the ten major trade unions operating in the seventeen Lucas factories throughout the United Kingdom. In the course of their activities during the mid-1970s, the Lucas workers developed an approach so new within the labour movement that it has continued to have an inspirational effect, not only in the UK, but throughout the world. In 1976 the workers produced a statement of their objectives in the form of a Corporate Plan:

"The objective of the plan is two-fold. Firstly to protect our members right to work by proposing a range of alternative products on which they could become engaged in the event of further cutbacks in the aerospace industry. Secondly, to ensure that amongst the alternative products proposed are a number which will be socially useful to the community." (1)

The Plan suggested that a product, method, and technology has social use in so far as it embodied a definite set of objectives. These include: the conservation of non-renewable resources; the enhancement of job control, skill, and knowledge; increased co-operation between intellectual and manual labour, and the pooling of skills; increased democratic control over production by the workforce, the users, and the community; and a reduction in the separation between producer and consumer, along with the encouragement of joint planning of the uses of technology. While the Lucas workers did not succeed in persuading the management of Lucas to implement their ideas, the concept of popular planning and workers' plans has become part of the currency of debate among trade unions and others seeking to extend the idea and practice of the social control and design of new technologies.

While Mike Cooley and the Lucas workers devoted their energies to the products of the industrial system, Bill Mollison was concerned about developing operational alternatives to the techniques of agriculture and of land-use. Just as the Lucas initiative concentrated attention on the skills and knowledge needed for socially useful technologies, Mollison applied himself to the design of techniques for a sustainable agriculture. Having taught environmental studies at Hobart in Tasmania, Mollison left the academic world, and in 1979 he established the Permaculture Institute. Permaculture (perennial culture or permanent agriculture) aims to evolve a system of agriculture which does not over-exploit and destroy its own natural resources (water, soil, forests, etc.). A basic principle of permaculture is contained in the idea that the stability of an ecosystem is related to diversity. Mollison, in his book 'Permaculture Two', acknowledges that other people have developed similar ideas to his own, and that much of the work of permaculture is to rediscover lost wisdom:

"Perhaps Fukuoka, in his book 'The One Straw Revolution', has best stated the basic philosophy of permaculture. In brief it is a philosophy of working with, rather than against, nature; of protracted and thoughtful observation, rather than protracted and thoughtless labour; and of looking at plants and animals in all their functions, rather than treating any area as a single product system".

Permaculture therefore never exploits a site for a single product. Rather, the purpose of site design is to fit together the features of landscape, climate, plant and animal species, buildings, and humans, into a stable and productive system. Permaculture teaches the de-industrialisation of agriculture, the return to a diversity of skills and crops. However, the system is not only intended for application to farming.

Mollison has advocated the applicability of intensive gardening in urban settings.

Mollison's first two books were widely influential when published in 1978 and 1979. (2) In the books the practicalities of design and application are detailed, but the underlying philosophy is also made clear:

"I believe that the days of centralised power are numbered . . . the applied theories of politics, economics, and industry have made a sick society; it is time for new approaches. We live in a post-industrial world, and have an immense amount of information and technology which enables us to exchange information while living in a village situation . . .

Permaculture both conserves and generates the fuel energies of transport systems, and would enable any community to exist comfortably on very restricted land areas. Supplemented with the appropriate and available technologies of methane and alcohol fuels, dry distillation processes, and wind, water, and solar energies, it would provide the basis of a sustainable and regionalised society. Combined with community co-operation, permaculture promises freedom from many of the ills that plague us, and accepts all the organic wastes of the community it serves". (3)

Mollison has worked with Australian aborigines, and has used some of the wisdom of this old culture to guide the techniques of permaculture. In the same way, Hassan Fathy has drawn upon the knowledge embodied in the traditional architectural heritage and in the craft skills of Egypt to design and build housing for people which combines economic, social, and aesthetic considerations. Hassan Fathy taught at the Faculty of Fine Arts in Cairo, serving as head of its architecture section. His experience is related in his book 'Architecture for the Poor' (1973), which tells the story of the building of the village of New Gournia in the Nile Valley, and which shows that it is possible to build for the poor both cheaply and humanly, by drawing on resources of cooperative self help, combined with the skills and techniques of the architect:

"A village society takes long to measure and needs more subtle instruments than a tape measure. One thing was clear from the start: that each family must be designed for separately . . ." (4)

Dr Fathy's book describes in detail how he went about this objective and developed an architecture which revived local crafts and decorative arts; which broke the dependence on structural steel and concrete; and which brings a human centered architecture within the reach of the poor.

Notes:

1. Statement from Lucas Aerospace Joint Shop Stewards Combine Committee, 1976.

2. 'Permaculture One—A Perennial Agriculture for Human Settlements', (1978); and 'Permaculture Two—Practical Designs for Town and Country in Permanent Agriculture', (1979)

3. See the article on Permaculture by Penny Strange, in The Ecologist, Vol. 13, nos. 2-3, 1983.

4. H. Fathy, 'Architecture for the Poor', (1973), p.51.

LUCAS AND SOCIALLY USEFUL PRODUCTION

Mike Cooley

9th December 1981

ONE OF THE major contradictions now confronting our so called technologically advanced societies is the gap between that which technology could provide for society, and that which it actually does provide for society.

The science and technology of the military industrial complex, in which I've worked for twenty years, can now produce guidance systems so incredibly sophisticated that we can aim a missile system on to an entirely different continent with a degree of accuracy of a few millimetres; but the blind and the lame in our society still stumble across roads in rather the same way as they did in medieval times. We have got recognition systems which can identify an enemy missile thousands of miles away, but we are incapable of recognizing the real enemies in our midst: the squalor, the disease and the filth which results in something like six hundred million people throughout this planet starving.

Probably the ultimate in our weapon sophistication is that we can now produce (and are producing) weapon systems which will destroy human beings and will leave property intact; yet we are incapable of eliminating poverty even here in metropolitan Europe. A recent EEC report suggests that something like thirteen million people in the EEC are undernourished, and in the Third World it's much worse.

It is a measure of the depravity of the whole value system of our society that in countries like Britain fifty per cent of our scientists and technologists spend their lifetime working on weapon systems, which they know in their heart of hearts would, if they were ever used, probably mean the end of humanity as we now know it.

Even when we get the so-called spin-offs from the military industrial complex, we end up with something as sophisticated as Concorde. Yet that very same society allows old age pensioners to die of hypothermia, because they cannot get a simple, effective, heating system. The spin-off from the guidance systems and the communication networks for the missiles have meant that we can send messages around the world in fractions of a second, but it now takes longer to send an ordinary letter from Washington to New York than it did in the days of the stagecoach. By using some of the most advanced interactive graphic techniques from the aero-dynamic side of the armaments industry, we can optimise car bodies so that they are aero-dynamically stable at about 180 km.p.h. when the average speed of a car through the centre of New York is now 11 km.p.h. It was 16 km.p.h. at the turn of the century when they were horsedrawn.

It was in an attempt to reverse this sad history that the Lucas workers drew up the corporate plan. I would firstly like to describe to you the scale and nature of the company so that you get some idea of the kind of forces you have to face when you engage on an enterprise of this kind.

Lucas Aero-Space is owned by a vast multi-national corporation employing seventy five thousand people in the UK, and something like thirty five thousand abroad. It's development in recent years has been characterised firstly by a shift of capital into Europe, so much so that the French government had to enact specific legislation to prevent Lucas monopolizing parts of their production. Even nation states now feel themselves threatened by these vast corporations. The company has been expanding rapidly into those parts of the world where labour is badly organised, and where there are resources which can be exploited and developed. The Aero-Space division which I shall be describing, began towards the end of the 1960s to take over a whole range of smaller companies. This was a form of rationalization which has been repeated in ship-building in Sweden, in the automotive industry in W. Germany and elsewhere. Some of the factories were small, quite flexible plants, employing about 300 people. Others were large dedicated plants, employing something like 3,000 people. They grouped them all together and they ended up with a national configuration of seventeen plants throughout the UK, employing something like 18,000 workers in the Aero-Space division.

It was clear to us that the company was going to rationalize that set-up out of existence, close down some of the plants, and set one against the other. In order that they could not do that, we established an organisation which is still unique in the British Labour and Trade Union movement. It is called the Lucas Aero-Space Combine Shop Stewards Committee, and it links together the highest level technologists in the company with the people on the shop floor. Thus you have in one organisation the analytical power of the scientist and the technologist linked together with what in my experience is more important: the common sense of people who work on the shop floor.

Before we could get that organisation properly established, we formed our own small newspaper, so that the workforce had an alternative source of information, rather than having to depend on management. It very rapidly developed into quite an extensive newspaper which now goes to all our plants, and informs people through their own network exactly what is happening in the other plants.

Before we could get the Committee properly going, the company said it was going to close an old plant in a working class area of London. There were about 1,500 people working there (in 1972). We occupied the plant, even the laboratories;

we prevented the company taking equipment in or out, but we were simply campaigning for the right to produce the same old products in the same old way. The work force couldn't see where all this was leading, and their morale had so declined by the sixth weekend that they didn't occupy it on Saturday and Sunday. The company heard that, they called in a demolition group, they tore the roof off the factory, they took the high capital equipment out and then set the building on fire to demolish it. Now I don't know about Sweden, but there is much said in Britain about vandalism, by which is meant a few children having a punch-up at a football match; but as far as we were concerned this was vandalism of an infinitely greater order, which had snatched from us overnight the sole means by which we express ourselves economically and otherwise.

So we were totally defeated. I think it is important when you've been defeated either in your private life or in your community or in whichever group you belong to, that you look realistically at that defeat, and you analyze it and see how you can handle it more creatively next time around. In the discussion arising out of that disaster, one worker asked an elegantly simple question. He said "Why can we not use the skills and abilities that we've got to meet the interests of the community as a whole? Why can we not produce socially useful products which will help human beings rather than maim them?"

The first stage in that process was to get the workforce to begin to analyze its own skills and abilities. The process I now describe, in my view, could be applied to any city, to any industry, or to any part of a country, or indeed to a total country itself.

The work-force began to go out and look at what was going on in the different workshops and laboratories. They found that we had high temperature, high pressure test facilities—climate chambers in which we can simulate conditions in near or outer space. We have got one of the most highly skilled workforces in the UK, although I would argue that skill in the sense of technical skill really had nothing to do with what happened. Some of the most exciting things that are happening are amongst unskilled and de-skilled people.

We were producing a range of equipment from high precision mechanical equipment, to highly stressed but lightweight sections for the RB 2-11 engines, (complete gas turbines including all the gears and equipment); and we also have our own electronics industry, where the airborne computers are produced to control the aircraft systems.

This was the first time in their lives that the Lucas workers actually realized what was going on in the different workshops, what was going on in the different laboratories. In Britain we are conditioned to view the world through the one machine we operate, or the one desk from which we function. Never are we encouraged to take a panoramic view of our industry, or see how that industry relates to other people and to other requirements.

Having collected all of this data, we then did what society conditions people like us to do. We asked 180 experts what they thought we could be doing with that skill and ability. We wrote to university professors who had given profound lectures in the monastic quiet of the universities; we wrote to intellectuals who had written massive books about how science and technology should be made relevant; we wrote to every professional body in the UK; we wrote to the bureaucracies of all the major trade unions. Out of all those 180 world authorities, only three were able to say anything that was remotely useful. From the rest of them we got vague generalizations. Some of them said 'If you refer to my paper of 1972 in Boston, ref. 32 is relevant to the problem you wish to address.' Nothing specific around which industrial workers could organize themselves to cope with the real problems which were grinding in on top of them.

We then did what we should have done in the first

instance. We asked our own workforce what they thought they could and should be doing. We arranged discussions in all the factories, and then we followed this up with a unique questionnaire to elicit the information and creativity which I will describe in a moment. These were sociologists from both the left and the right, and one of them said to us, 'One thing you should always remember is to design the questionnaire so that the consciousness of the person filling it in is not changed.' They said 'It is inadmissible as a research methodology to change the consciousness of those involved. You should be an objective researcher from outside examining the phenomena in a scientific way.'

We sought to do precisely the opposite. We deliberately structured the questionnaire so that those filling it in were caused to have their consciousness turned right on it's head. We asked them to think of themselves in their dual role in society, both as producers and as consumers, so that we transcended that ridiculous division which suggests that there is one nation that works in factories, offices and schools; and an entirely different nation that lives in houses and communities. We said that what you do during the day should be relevant to the way that you and your family would hope to live for the rest of your life.

Within six weeks, we had an incredible outpouring of creativity. We did not insist that people wrote great theses about the products they felt we could be making. I don't know about Sweden, but in Britain we confuse linguistic ability with intelligence. We are far more impressed by what people say and write than by what they do. In my experience, industrial workers express their intelligence by how they do things, how they organize them rather than how they talk about them. So we said to the workforce: 'If you wish to make models of the products you want, just go and make the models; if you want to talk about it, come and we'll talk about it.'

We have refined the 150 proposals we got into six product ranges, and I will briefly describe a few of them. We grouped these into six volumes where we describe each of the product ranges in some detail. The first product range is in the medical field. We were horrified to find that as part of the rationalization programme, the company was getting rid of two of the only socially useful products we were making. One was a pacemaker for people with weak hearts, the other one was a dialysis machine, a kidney machine. When we looked at the requirements for kidney machines in Britain, we were horrified to learn that every year 3,000 people die because they cannot get a kidney machine. In the Birmingham area the patients are allowed, as the consultant so nicely put it to us, 'to go into decline'.

If you're under fifteen or over forty five you are allowed to go 'into decline'. The same kind of problem exists in Sweden, W. Germany and the United States. To cut a long story short, we've now got a microprocessor in it so the patient can wear it on their back like a rucksack. They have the dignity of doing a worthwhile job rather than being acted upon like a piece of wood, which is frequently what Western medical technology does.

Another product we've designed is a vehicle for children with spina bifida. Now it's frequently asked where we are going to get the money to produce these products. Very seldom do we ask what is the cost of *not* making something. In modern industrial nations, if you put a worker out of work and they've got a couple of dependents, you have to pay them about sixty per cent of the average industrial wage. There is a loss of revenue to the nation state of about forty per cent. Add the two together and it's about one hundred per cent of the average industrial wage.

We went to the then Labour government and said 'Why could we not have this money and produce socially useful products?' Of course they were incapable of answering that, because it is so full of common sense that it is beyond the reason of politicians. We then looked at the social multipliers. You have the drug taking; the neuroses; the interpersonal violence; the illness which is directly related to unemployment. If you take all that into account, you get some measure of the cost to society as a whole of these large corporations, as they rationalize themselves and put more and more people out of work.

We do not believe that our society can go on wasting materials and energy in the way in which it is now doing, and we have designed a whole range of energy conserving systems. One of them is a heat pump which runs on natural gas, in an internal combustion engine. You can get 2.8 times as much useful energy in the house as you would get if you burn it directly, and about twice as much as you would get if you were driving the unit by electricity. Lucas said that they would not produce these as they were incompatible with their product range and would not be profitable. We intercepted a secret company report which showed that the market for these would be something like £1,000,000,000, in the EEC countries by 1986. But Lucas would not produce them because that would mean admitting that the workforce was able to say what could be made, how it should be made, and in whose interest. You see, we're dealing not just with a economic system; we are also dealing with a political system which is concerned about demonstrating its power and holding on to that power.

We have also designed a hybrid power-pack for cars, coaches or trains. You may or may not know that the engine in your car is about four times bigger than it need be, to give you take-off torque, that is to get the car going. Once you've got it moving a very much smaller one would do. On the other hand an electric motor has got a high starting torque, so we've linked the two together to create a hybrid power-pack. All the energy you waste as you idle at traffic lights, as you start cold in the morning, as you are caught in traffic jams—is all going in as useful energy into the system. You can reduce energy consumption by fifty per cent and toxic emissions, the poisonous gases, by about eighty per cent.

But what is unique about this is that we've designed it with bolted construction, carefully selecting the materials and increasing bearing sizes so that it is capable of running, with suitable maintainance, for about twenty years. And you can actually maintain it, it's deliberately designed so that you could repair it. Now some people said 'If you do that it would cause unemployment.' We had a gut feeling that if you designed so that you could repair it, there would be as much work repairing it as you would have on mass production lines producing on a throw away basis.

There has been a report from the Batelle Institute in Geneva which shows that if you design cars and engines to last for twenty years, not only would you conserve energy and materials, but you would create sixty five per cent more work. And the work you would create would be the interesting, diagnostic, fiddling type of work that human beings love doing, rather than the grotesque alienated work that you get on production lines. These are real options that are open to us!

We would like to see the hybrid power pack built into a unique vehicle we have designed, which we call a Hybrid Road-Rail vehicle, and which is capable of running as a bus (on normal roads), and also running on a railway line on particular branch lines. In order to design this vehicle, and even to think of it, it was necessary for us to look at different levels of reality of technology. The first level of reality of the transport systems is the ad man's version of the car. The car is always new and gleaming; it will typically have a power-pack in it four times bigger than it need have, to give you peak velocity which you cannot even use on a motorway. You are given the impression that you're letting yourself and your family down if you don't have a new one every two or three years, and it is usually designed, around the wheel arches, or maybe the subframe, to ensure that it will begin to fall apart after two or three years. It's always shown in a rural setting, the beautiful countryside, the ideal being that it liberates you at the evening and the weekends from the squalor you've spent the rest of your time producing.

The second order of reality is what this is doing to our cities, shaking antique buildings apart, polluting the centres. The third order of reality is the tragic wastage of energy and materials of all kinds. One could do an energy count of the sheet steel, the glass, the rubber. Suffice to say that if you throw away a car under 80,000 miles, or ten years, whichever comes first, you are throwing away the amount of energy that would be required to drive it.

But worst of all, it seems to us, is the waste of the lives of the human beings who, day in day out, have got to degrade themselves on production lines producing that sort of throw-away rubbish.

In designing the Road-Rail vehicle, we deliberately did not make a virtue of complexity. In the aero-space industry, and the military industrial complexes, we love to make everything complex, and I'm a stress analyst myself, and can make most things look complex. We normally use very long mathematical formulae; we then test the thing out in reality. We still end up with a big formula, which means that we look very profound, but it also means that practical workers on the shop floor just don't know what's going on.

In this case we deliberately didn't do it that way at all. We asked a skilled worker what size he thought the axle should be. He said 35 millimetres; we made it 35 millimetres and it's functioning perfectly—and of course it is, because that person had spent a lifetime making axles and components. In other words we were utilising that precious tacit knowledge which Polanyi described when he said: "They are things we know but cannot tell". By using this practical knowledge it is possible to democratise decision-making within the design process, and involve masses of so-called ordinary people.

We then collected money throughout the factories and bought an old coach. We took out the steering mechanism and, in the unique centre we've set up the North East

London Polytechnic, we assembled it and we tested it on the Sussex railway line. It functioned perfectly. Now this has become our sort of technological agit-prop. We can now travel any place throughout the country, on either road or rails. We've got video tapes and slides inside, so that we can stop in communities and people can really see how you could begin to move towards an integrated ecologically desirable transport system. When there are demonstrations against unemployment, this vehicle leads the parade as an example of the kind of things people could be doing.

We also produced the hob-cart, for children with spina bifida. I should point out that this very simple little product was designed by Mike Parry Evans, one of the leading systems designers in the world. He said that when he took this little cart down to a five year old child, and saw the pleasure on the child's face, that meant far more to him than all the abstract problems we deal with in the military industrial complex. For the first time he actually saw a person who was going to use the product he had designed, and he was physically in contact with the problem because he had to make a clay mold of the child's back. Lucas refused to produce these hobcarts because they were 'incompatible' with their product range! Some 500 have now been produced in a Borstal—a prison for young people. Some of the social workers there have pointed out the extraordinary humanising effect this has had on the young prisoners.

At the beginning of the 1800s in the USA there used to be 86% of the population working in agriculture. Gradually that has been automated, so that they now even have tractors which can find their way around the field, and four per cent now produce an agricultural output many times greater than before automation. But the energy you get from the food so produced is actually less than the energy input if you take into account the tractors, the harvesters, and the chemicals. Likewise in manufacturing with automation; for example, in the case of the telephone industry where it used to take twenty six workers to produce one unit of equivalent switching power. With first generation electronics it will be ten, soon it will be one. But I don't think anybody can seriously suggest that it's going to be possible to increase production by twenty six times. We are confusing productivity and production. In our view we are going to see the cyclical basis of unemployment going up, and the base of unemployment continuing to rise, and the jobs vacant going down, so that the gap between the two gets bigger and bigger. There is now talk in one of the latest EEC reports that there could be 20,000,000 people out of work in the EEC countries by 1988. And as unemployment grows, so it will be said that we must have more armaments industries, as a way of overcoming the problems of unemployment.

It is vital that we point out that there are real alternatives, and that work is important to human beings. I don't mean grotesque alienated work, but work in it's historical context, which needs hand and brain in a meaningful productive process. If you ask anybody what they are, they will never say I'm a Beethoven lover, a Bob Dylan fan or a James Joyce reader, (it's perhaps a pity that they don't) but they say I'm a fitter, a turner, a teacher, a nurse or whatever. We relate to society and to other people by the work we do, and we learn and develop as we work on the world about us.

It used to be argued that, while where is unemployment, eventually the new jobs which emerge from the new technology will be that much more fulfilling, exciting and interesting. A whole range of industrial sociologists have said this. We have examined what has been happening when you introduce the most advanced numerically controlled equipment, and we found it to be incredibly de-skilling. There has recently been a report from the 'American Machinist' in the United States, a leading technical paper, which says that the ideal worker at these machines should have a mental age of twelve, and, as one American sociologist put it, if they weren't mentally retarded when they went in, they certainly will be when they come out.

There's a whole area of concern now amongst computer scientists, that we are becoming so separated from the real world that we're begining to fail to recognise the actual world we're working on. But there is another, much more complex problem, as the human being interacts with this kind of equipment. The human being is the dialectical opposite of the machine. If we speak in systems terms, the human being is slow, inconsistent, unreliable, but highly creative. The machine is fast, consistent, reliable and totally non-creative. The system can handle the quantitative elements so fast that the decision rate of the designer can be forced up by 1800% as he attempts to keep pace, and deal with the qualitative judgements.

We find that the interaction is so great that the creativity of the worker is reduced by thirty per cent in the first hour, by eighty per cent in the second hour, thereafter, they are exhausted. They're now working out the response time of intellectual workers, using this kind of equipment. They give them tasks of varying complexity and they work out the response rate. The've discovered that as you get older, so you get slower. Now I knew that as a child of five, when I looked at my grandparents.

Having collected all of the data, they then worked out the peak performance ages for different groups of workers. They found that a mathematician would reach his or her peak performance at the age of 24-25. For a theoretical physicist it's a little later, 26-27. Right the way through the spectrum to the mechanical engineer—apparently we're the most durable of all, at 34, which means I'm thirteen years beyond my peak performance age. They then say we should have a careers plateau, and thereafter a careers de-escalation. The point I want to make to you here is that not only does this kind of technology burn up energy and materials, it also burns up human beings. The shape of that performance curve is exactly the same as that which existed at earlier historical stages. Manual workers for example could reach their peak prowess when they were 18. They could stand the pressure for about ten years, and thereafter were burned up. If you look at the rate at which manual workers are required to work in modern industry, you get some idea of what has been happening to them. In one of the most highly automated and computerized plants in Europe, there is an agreement that the workforce will have as its rest period 32.4 minutes, and the elements that make that up are as follows: trips to the lavatory 1.62 mins (it's computer precise, it's not 1.6 or 1.7, it's 1.62 mins); recovery from fatigue 1.3 mins; sitting down after standing too long 65 seconds; from monotony 32 seconds, and so the grotesque litany goes on. That is the price we are paying at the point of production for our throw-away cars, and the kind of infrastructures which we're building. But we are also dramatically de-humanising people within industry. It is now said that with advanced computer systems, we should no longer think of human beings; we should think of human materials.

That which is most precious about human beings, the ability to think for themselves, is now said to be an attribute which should be suppressed by technology. It seems to me entirely consistent that the military industrial complex, which says that you should think of human materials, not human beings, can then quite easily take that little extra step and say it's all right to eliminate human beings with the neutron bomb and leave property intact.

The last three points I want to make are these. As the problems I've described get worse and worse, more technology is produced to solve the problems. One of the big diversification programmes in a French aero-space company has been to produce a 'bolt-hole'. Those of you who know about nature will know that that's what a rabbit runs to when it's terrified. Using the most advanced techniques of sealing and silencing, they've produced this absolutely soundproof capsule. Depending on your level of neurosis, your psychiatrist can prescribe music, so you can lock yourself away in your own little private personal padded cell. In other words, you seal yourself off from the problems of society, rather than confronting them directly.

I understand that these are selling in their hundreds to neurotic executives in France. It's even portable, so you can take it out in the countryside, and you're not even disturbed by the birds and the bees!

Secondly, on the front page of our corporate plan we make a major point that we hope we will see more women in science and technology. We looked at one of the leading computer journals over a period of eighteen months, and 82% of the adverts that showed one person with equipment, showed a young dolly bird type person, the male image of what a woman should be like. In other works, the idea that women are play-things that you have around to sell the equipment. We say on the front page of our corporate plan, that if only more women would come into science and technology, not as imitation men, or as honorary males, (because equality can never mean sameness), but to point out that our Western science and technology is dominated by the predominantly male value system, the value system of the white, male, capitalist, warrior hero. It would be an incredible philosophical contribution if we inject into science and technology the so-called female attributes of intuition, subjectivity and humanity.

The last point I want to make is that science and technology is not given. It is not like the sun or the moon or the stars. It was made by people like us. If it's not doing for us what we want, we have a right and a responsibility to change it. Increasingly we have been conditioned to believe that we should change ourselved to suit the technology, and it's been done in all sorts of subtle ways. There is a very famous advert in Britain showing a woman suffering from what technology has done to her. She's suffering from 'high-rise blues' and the advert says very subtly that she cannot change her environment, (and I would ask why not) but it goes on to say that you can change her mood with a tranquilliser. Now it's not pills and tranquillisers we need, but a clear view of what we want from science and technology, and the courage to stand up and do something about it.

It's frequently asked of me, 'Do you really think that ordinary people can deal with these problems?' I personally have never met an ordinary person in my life. All the people I meet are extraordinary. They've got all kinds of skills, abilities and talents, and never are those talents used or developed or encouraged. What we've got to remember, as we're driven down this linear road of technology, is that the future is not 'out there' someplace, as America was out there before Columbus went to discover it. The future has not got pre-determined shapes and forms. The future has yet got to be built by people like you and I, and we do have real choices. It can be a future in which we are not threatened with mass annihilation through nuclear weapons, or ravaged with hunger. It could really be a world in which we treasure all our people equally, and get science and technology to serve people rather than the other way round. In a word, we should begin to perform the modern miracle, we could help to make the blind see, the lame walk, and we could feed the hungry.

PERMANENT AGRICULTURE

Bill Mollison

9th December 1981

I GREW up in a small village in Tasmania. I was born in 1928, but my village might have existed in the eleventh century. We didn't have any cars; everything that we needed we made. We made our own boots, our own metal works, we caught fish, grew food, made bread. I didn't know anybody who lived there who had one job, or anything that you could define as a job. Everybody had several jobs.

As a child I lived in a sort of a dream and I didn't really awaken until I was about 28. I spent most of my working life in the bush or on the sea. I fished, I hunted for my living. It wasn't until the 1950s that large parts of the system in which I lived were disappearing. First, fish stocks became extinct. Then I noticed the seaweed around the shorelines had gone. Large patches of forest began to die. I hadn't realised until those things were gone that I'd become very fond of them, that I was in love with my country. This is about the last place I want to be; I would like to be sitting in the bush watching wallabies. However, if I don't stand here, there will be no bush and no wallabies to watch. The Japanese have come to take away most of our forest. They are using it for newsprint. I notice that you are putting it in your waste-paper basket. That's what has happened to the life systems I grew up in.

It's always a mark of danger to me when large biological

systems start to collapse, when we lose whole stocks of fish, as we've lost whole stocks of herring, and many stocks of sardines, when we lose huge areas of the sea bottom which were productive in scallops and oysters. When we enquire why this happens, it comes back to one thing: the use of energy sources not derived from the biological system.

Dr. Sternglass, who was a pupil of Einstein's, has followed the drift of radioactive dust from Three Mile Island. The newspapers say: 'Nobody died at Three Mile Island'. Dr. Sternglass says that 30,000 children are now dead, under the cloud drifts of hypothyroidosis, and many thousands are yet to die. Across this country, Russia, Germany, Japan, Canada and the United States, drifts an air system, carrying not only radioactives, but highly corrosive acids: sulphuric acids from the burning of coal, and nitric acids from motor vehicle exhausts.

The snow which we measured in Vermont a few months ago had ph values of 1.9 to 2.5, which is more acid than vinegar, more acid than any biological system can stand. We cannot find in the Northern part of the United States or in Germany waters of ph higher than 4. Fish can't breed in those waters, frogs can't live there, and salamanders are extinct. Forests started to die in 1920, soon after the coal era started. Chestnuts have disappeared on the American continent by 80%; the beech trees have disappeared. The oaks are beginning to die throughout America, the pines are dying in Germany (they're losing 80,000 hectares this year) and many of them are now dying in Japan. The Eucalyptus are dying in Australia at 14% per annum. It won't be very long before you won't have any forests to throw away in your garbage cans! It's obvious to simple people like myself, who go out on foot to find out what's happening, that the Northern hemisphere will not be occupied by man for very many more years while he uses coal, petrol and radioactives. I wonder what happened to make us abandon the sort of life that I grew up in, in which we could sustain our lives indefinitely and in which no great systems died. I don't believe that we lead a better life, that we are any happier than I was and the children in that town still are.

I withdrew from society about 1970 because I had been long in opposition to the systems that I saw were killing us. I decided it was no good persisting with opposition that got you nowhere. I thought for two years. I wanted to return to society but I wanted to come back only with something very positive. I did not want to oppose anything again and waste my time. Somewhere someone had given me Mao Tse Tung's Little Red Book. I didn't understand it very well, in fact it was very difficult for me to read but, at one point when he was talking about an attack on the city of Tai Ching, his advice to his army was 'Don't attack Tai Ching: it's too heavily defended. Go around it and Tai Ching will fall.' So I've been going around the things that I think are killing us.

When I came back into society I came back with a system I call Permaculture, a way in which man can live on the earth. To me we're not any more important a form of life than any other life form. Those of you, very few, who have been alone in forests for a long time, more than five weeks, know that you totally lose identity as a human being. You can't distinguish yourself from the trees, you can't distinguish yourself from any other living thing there. All aboriginal people, all tribal people, have to undergo such a period on their own in the environment. Afterwards, they never again can see themselves as separate: man here and tree there. You become as though you are simply a part of life.

The only safe energy systems are those derived from biological systems. A New Guinea gardener can walk through the gates of his garden taking one unit of energy, and hand out seventy. A modern farmer who drives a tractor through the gate of his farm takes a thousand units of energy in and gives one back. Who is the most sophisticated agriculturalist? We are getting rid of our soil even faster than we are destroying our atmosphere. For every one of us there is a loss of ten tons of soil a year! Nature can only replace one or two tons. We will leave our children an earth in which there is no soil or drinkable water.

We ourselves have always been left out of the energy equations. I'm the only machine I know which can fuel itself: I can make the food upon which I run. Give me a few friends and I can look after myself and many others. This will do me for an alternative energy source. We've never been taught to have confidence in ourselves as our own salvation. All the books you can buy on gardening are books on technique. All the books on strategy are wrong because they are one-dimensional. Multi-dimensional systems will out-yield one-dimensional systems hundreds of times. Polycultures will always out-yield monocultures. The Permaculture system is a safe way of a sustained ecology; it is in itself a safe and sustainable energy system.

In the days of Carl Linnaeus we were still naming things. For a century or so after Linnaeus we were finding out how they functioned. Today we know some of the principles that make them work, but, just as we've reached this stage, they have commenced to fall apart. We estimate that of the species that we can see and count, we will lose some 35,000 in the next one and a half decades. All my life we've been at war against nature. I just pray that we lose that war. There are no winners in that war.

A couple of years ago I resigned from a job at the university and threw myself at an advanced age into an uncertain future. I decided to do nothing else but to try to persuade people to build good biological systems. I existed for quite a while by catching fish and pulling potatoes. Then I started to make some money by designing sustainable systems for people, for their own houses and for their villages. Since then I've been able to train 20 people at a time. I have trained 400 young people who are now designing systems throughout the U.S. and Australia. In the coming year I will be training people in Germany and Brazil. We've set up a sort of brotherhood—and sisterhood, because half of us are women. I don't believe women are any better designers than men, but I think they know more about living systems.

We must make a very large movement towards a very quiet sort of revolution. We will go on training people until we have saturated all countries. What we try to do is to integrate all things that plants and animals will do, with our own lives and our structures. It's possible to design entirely biological systems in which you could live, but we have to start with a place like Stockholm, which is about as abiological as you can get. There are simple things that anybody can do to look after themselves. Every city, for example, can produce its own food.

We are faced with an absolute choice: we can build the sort of cities we are building, continue to accumulate resources and power to run around like blowflies in cars, and be killed before long. Or we can live easily on the earth. It's possible for us to construct biological systems that work, it's well within our capacity. For a fraction of the cost of Swedish armaments, Sweden could become an entire system like this. It's up to you, it's entirely up to you. I hope you all go back to work tomorrow and take your wages. Good luck to you.

PEOPLE'S ARCHITECTURE
Dr. Hassan Fathy
9th December 1980

WE NEED a new way of knowledge. The enforced academic knowledge of schools has alienated us from nature, just as industrialisation by force has taken away the possibilities of our participating in satisfying our needs. We have only ready-made solutions, prefabricated ideas to be carried out. In the fields of life which need a high cash outlay, like housing, we have been cut off from solving our problems by using our own hands and own potential. We have been integrated into the cash economy. By this integration we have imposed on the poor the cash economy without the cash. The annual income per capita in the Third World is between £25 and £30. How can someone with such an income hire an architect and a contractor to build his house for him with industrialised materials which need cash? Imposing the cash economy on these people has created a class I call the economic untouchables, because they cannot be integrated into the cash economy and have been deprived from doing anything themselves. The effect of this is that, according to U.N. statistics, 20 years ago there were 800 million people in the Third World doomed to a premature death because of bad housing alone, not to mention nutrition and other needs. I thought that this figure must have surpassed the billion by now. But they tell me it is 'only' 900 million.

The system prevailing now is the architect/contractor

system by which the owner has been completely set aside, as the architect designs and the contractor builds. To solve the problem of the 900 million we have to have not low cost housing but no cost housing. We must subject technology and science to the economy of the penniless, the people, instead of the other way round. This is the role of the conscious modern architect, this is our great responsibility. Up to now many governments and international organisations have tried to solve the problem by trying to find some means of reducing the costs of building and of the industrialized materials. They have produced what they call aided self-help for the Third World, by providing concrete shakers and vibrators to make prefabricated panels for building. But after twenty years of experimenting with this system thay have had to confess that it does not work. Because a man with an income of £25 a year cannot afford any industrialised materials like cement and concrete. The problem is not in the shaker and the vibrator, the problem is what to shake and vibrate. We have to rely on the materials we have and can afford to have, on our labour, on our own hands, on what we find under our feet. Nature itself has provided the solution. The cave men noticed, after threshing corn, that straw mixed with earth makes big lumps which hold together. The earth molecules do not hold together enough so we have to have a stabilising factor. The straw mixed with mud at harvest time showed man how to make mud bricks, Adobe, to build walls. When he came to the problem of roofing, primitive man used timber or other materials. But timber was not always at hand.

In Iran, Egypt, Libya and Tunisia they found a solution. If you build a boat, every ring is pulling on the other, and it is working entirely under tension. There is no compression or it would crumble. If you reverse this upwards it will be working entirely under compression. Mud brick can take compression but not tension. They invented a system to build roofs with just bricks end to end, leaning the vertical a little against an end wall so that the brick is on an incline plane. The sticking power is the weight of the brick multiplied by the cosign of the angle divided by the area of the brick. They found that they had to have very light adobe bricks, 25cm by 15cm and only 5cm thick.

Once all this is recognised, modern science can help by giving us the qualities of mud, the physical, mechanical qualities and so on, and even solve the problem that mud brick does not last long in more humid areas through stabilisation with bituminous emulsions.

Those who want to play with mud-bricks ought to be a trio. The cellist would be the soil engineer deeply in tune with the vibrations of the soil. The violinist, highly strung, would be the structural engineer. The architect would be the conductor. We can use mud-brick adobe, which costs nothing except the hand labour, with the same security as steel and concrete. We have examples which have lasted from antiquity. Bolting goes back in history to the very earliest period. The first example I know in Egypt is from the Third Dynasty, something like 5,000 years ago. They used the parabolic bolt as a centering and built an arch. We have another example in an oasis in Upper Egypt. In the fourth century A.D. the Christians were persecuted by the Romans, and a group fled into the desert. They had nothing, only what was under their bare feet, but they built something like 250 structures, all vaulted with domes, using mud-brick from under their feet. These models are still standing. The 'experts' say that mud-brick would not last and the maintenance costs would be astronomical, due to the fragility of the mud. But these buildings have been studied by architects and engineers.

To my mind the value of any project, any ideas, lies in the answer to the question: is it for people or for politics, economics, etc? When we think about housing people, we have to think about the quality of life of the people, we have to think about the quality of life of the people we are serving. For example, when you have 20 people sleeping in one room the airing requirements are different. We have to consider the aesthetic factor. When they were working with their own hands men used to beautify everything they made. Even if it was a warship it was carved with the most fantastic designs because man was interacting with the wood. But machinery does not care for beauty.

It takes time for certain changes to show their effects. If we could jump from the sixth floor and our legs would not break until six months later, we would have many people with broken legs because they would not associate cause with effect! Some of the mistakes we commit need time to reveal themselves. If a family of five can farm five acres, and somebody gives them a tractor and a mechanical plough so they can farm twenty times five acres, it is seen as progress. But we have dispensed with nineteen other families. What are they going to do for a living? We have dispensed with the plough carpenter, the village weaver and all the crafts that were being satisfied in the village. The tractor does not eat from the ground like the cow, or give milk, nor does it give any manure, only poisonous gases. It needs fuel and spare parts and changes the economy of the countryside. God created man in Nature surrounded by plant and animal life. In our cities we have only asphalt, steel, aluminium and concrete. The best material you can surround yourself with when considering cosmic radiation is wood. The worst is concrete which stops the beneficial radiation. Water is affected by the cosmic rays coming from the moon and as our bodies are almost all liquid, all water, they are affected too. But we never think about these things. Modern man has lost this cosmic consciousness. The cathedrals of France were built on the geographical area reflecting the sign of the Virgin in the sky reflected on earth. Why? We are part of a system. If I integrate myself into the system all the elements in the system will come to help me. If I cut my finger all the elements of my body will come to heal it. But if my finger were isolated it would never heal.

How do we go from the architect/contractor system to the architect-owner/builder system? This needs quite a change in the relationships between the people concerned. In the communities with £25 per head income, nothing can explain their remaining alive, unless they live outside the cash economy, depending mainly on co-operation. One man cannot build a house, but ten men can build ten houses very easily, even a hundred houses. We need a system that allows the traditional way of co-operation to work in our society. I cannot co-operate in a city if the moment I get out of the door I am launched into the anonymity of millions. We must create new neighbourhoods where I build for you and you build for me (i.e. I will have the same help from you when I come to build my house).

What a waste of energy not to use our muscles properly for building, for culture, for modelling beauty! When I think of the energy wasted on football: take a ball and run after it and have a goal and finito . . . If we could only make the millions have the same interest in construction as in football!

Instead of hatred and destruction we could have love and construction, because construction itself has that impact. Every act, anything we do has an impact on our basic nature. In the old societies they used to have the temple architecture reflecting the sky. So when the sun changed signs they would dismantle the temple and rebuild it according to the new measurements and directions! What is our standard of reference when we build? The findings of modern science, of physics? But we do not even take those into account. We put huge windows in the 'modern' houses we build in the desert nowadays, each one letting in thousands of kilo calories of heat an hour. They need a lot of air conditioning, a lot of cash, and when this cash runs out what will the people do with their houses and with themselves?

We must subject technology and science to the economy of the poor and penniless. We must add the aesthetic factor because the cheaper we build, the more beauty we should add to respect man. When man built on his own he used to beautify everything with his own hands. When architects build for the poor what do we give them from the aesthetic point of view? There is a book called 'Architecture without Architects'. When I see the present architecture, the regular architecture, I don't know which is which. Which is the architecture with or without the architect? Because we have over-simplified and over reduced our efforts, the modern house is the paid portrait of the owner. When we are designing for the rich we take care of the aesthetic factor, the functional and the demographic. But when we design for the 900 million, we design one house and have it multiplied by the million in Europe as it is in Africa, as it is in India and everywhere, because we are using concrete and concrete does not allow any manipulation of space or articulation of the material.

I would like to introduce in our villages and our cities musicality and harmonics. The eye physiologically does not see more than one point at a time, and sends these to the brain, one point after the other. We hear music, one note after the other, and have the melody in our brain. We have the image in our brain. It happens very quickly so we think it is instantaneous but it is not. When I look around a room my eyes go round the lines. If they are harmonic I feel happy. If they are hectic I feel nervous, but do not know why. I wish that the eye would suffer like the ear and when it sees ugliness become red and have tears! Unconsciously we feel the dissonance.

The material is amorphous, neutral. With half a cubic meter of clay, Rodin made the Thinker. The palaces of the Pharoahs were all in mud-brick. In New Mexico we have a style of architecture all in mud-brick from the time of the Indians. In Iran they have used a most interesting technique. I have seen a village school built in adobe covered by three vaults, one next to the other, to catch the breeze. The span was six metres! By combining the modern science of soil mechanics and structures, with the skill of master masons, we can have such vaulting in millions of houses. Instead, in hot humid zones, we get corrugated iron roofs that have to be paid for in cash and are not insulated from heat. We once invited all the architects and engineers in Egypt to present ideas for rural housing. Model buildings were put up in the grounds of the building research centre in Cairo. There was one entirely prefabricated, ultra modern, and one in mud-brick. Air temperatures in the prefabricated house were seven degrees centigrade higher than in the mud-brick one in April. The temperature in the mud-brick model didn't fluctuate more that two degrees in twenty four hours and never came out of the acceptable temperate zone. In the ultra-modern concrete model the temperature didn't enter into that temperate zone except during one hour in the morning and one hour in the evening. It was at times even higher than the outside temperature! So this 'modern' house ignored the findings of modern physics, aerodynamics, sociology, social psychology, physiology and so on. If you want to be modern, you have to consider all these sciences. In architecture, the human sciences are the most important.

This is what we mean by Right Livelihood. God has not changed the design of the face of man, having the nose above the mouth or in the back of the neck, just to be modern. When God created man out of mud-brick he asked the angels to bow down to Adam. They all bowed down, except Satan who wanted God to make man out of concrete!

CHAPTER FIVE

The Rights of People

The Rights of People

A GOOD measurement of the quality of life enjoyed by
people is the nature and variety of rights which they
enjoy. The Universal Declaration of Human Rights which
followed the ending of the Second World War stated that "the
advent of a world in which human beings shall enjoy freedom
of speech and belief and freedom from fear and want has been
proclaimed as the highest aspiration of the common people."
Theodoor Van Boven was Director of the United Nations
Division of Human Rights in Geneva from 1977 to 1982.
Since 1982 he has been Professor of Law at the University of
Limburg, Netherlands. He is also chairman of the European
Human Rights Foundation and of the Standing International
Forum on Ethnic Conflict, Development, and Human
Rights. His work amply illustrates the fundamental
importance of vigilance on human rights as a necessary
condition for human well-being. During his work with the
United Nations he sought to make UN concern with human
rights violations both consistent and comprehensive. He
attempted to break through the selective approach of the UN,
highlighting violations in a large number of countries on all
continents. At the same time he became concerned with such
issues as involuntary disappearances, torture, summary

execution, and discrimination against indigenous peoples. Van Boven not only sought to identify the violation of rights, but also their root causes in connection with, for example, the development process, with patterns of economic and political domination, with racial discrimination, and with the militarisation of societies. He was concerned to establish the notion of positive rights, and strongly favoured the right to development as a human right. In order to effectively fight for human rights, he called for a 'third system', that is the recognition of groups outside governmental and inter-governmental agencies, so that voices other than those of governments may be given greater prominence in the international system.

The Free Legal Assistance Volunteers Association (Free Lava) is precisely the kind of organisation to which Van Boven would like to give greater legitimacy and recognition. Free Lava works at the front line of human rights abuses, representing prisoners and detainees in prison in the Philippines under the regime of Marcos, conspicuous for its abuse of human rights. Winefreda Geonzon, for Free Lava, gives an account of the effective work which such an organisation can achieve. During her experience as a lawyer she became painfully aware of the widespread violations of human rights committed inside the jail at the city of Cebu in the Philippines. It was found by Free Lava volunteers, in their willingness to go into the prisons, that a great number of people were detained illegally and that atrocities against prisoners were frequent. However, the people who were the victims of these abuses were generally the people who could not afford to be legally represented. In its assistance of cases such as these, Free Lava performed a courageous service since not only were individual cases represented, but the officials responsible for abuse were identified and confronted. As well as free legal assistance, Free Lava promotes crime prevention programmes and assists prisoners to develop a sense of dignity.

The cultivation and protection of human rights means that public discussion of what constitutes legitimate freedoms and rights must be stimulated. Van Boven, as has been suggested above, saw that it was important to establish the right to development as a basic human right. It is in the practical recognition of this that the work of Lokayan in India is important. Lokayan (which means Dialogue with the People) was formed by Rajni Kothari in 1980. Kothari is also president of the Peoples Union for Civil Liberties, which was established during the state of emergency imposed by Indira Gandhi's government. At the same time there has been a terrific profusion of grass roots groups throughout India working on a variety of single issue affairs (including ecological issues, women's rights, the protection of ethnic minorities, the promotion of community development projects etc). Lokayan sees the importance of civil rights as an integrating issue, providing a common concern for the variety of grass roots groups. Lokayan has worked to form study groups and coordinate action around specific problem areas. Among the problems areas identified were the politics of oppression, specially the way in which discrimination and corruption has affected vulnerable groups like tribal peoples, harijans, and religious minorities. Secondly the problem of communal tensions has been specifically targeted for study and action. Thirdly, Lokayan has worked on the informal or unorganised labour sector, an area largely ignored by formal political parties and trade unions but which nevertheless, in the Indian context, is an extremely important one. Fourthly, Lokayan has concentrated on the problems of people in the tribal areas, looking especially at the effect of the forest policy of central and regional government, on the natural and human environment. In sum, Lokayan has sought to promote through dialogue between academics, professionals and ordinary people a new conception of human rights located in an alternative process of development.

In the Middle East the problems of human rights present

themselves in a different manner. Here the terrible impact of a state of almost continuous warfare, or preparation for war, between the state of Israel and surrounding Arab states, has shattered the security and daily lives of people, drawing them into a maelstrom of violence seemingly beyond their control. The Israeli invasion of the Lebanon in 1982, and the bombardment of Beirut, was the most recent of a series of major conflicts to hit the region. The impact of the war on ordinary Israelis has been traumatic. The impact of the war on Lebanon has been so dramatic that a virtual state of gun law has existed since. Yet the Middle East conflict is not merely a regional conflict; it has global significance, because it is the region most likely to trigger an escalation from conventional warfare to nuclear confrontation between the superpowers. Yet despite the awful threat which this possibility poses, human rights and peace movements internationally have not focussed their energies on the Middle East situation. In Lebanon, despite ten years of civil war and invasion, there has been little evidence of popular initiatives for peace. The initiative of Iman Khalife was important precisely because she decided that it was time that ordinary Lebanese people, who had been victims of the war, should proclaim their protest against it. Khalife was a school teacher in Beirut who had also carried out research on the effect of war on the moral judgement of children. Becoming increasingly angered by the violence in Lebanon, she responded by writing a poem which became a call to action to the citizens of Beirut to march for peace by gathering symbolically on the Green Line, which divides Moslem West from Christian East Beirut. The idea captured the imagination of thousands and was described by one young Lebanese as 'an expression of revolt by the common man against all the militias and against all the violence, which has become completely meaningless'.

The final two speeches in this collection deal with people who have contributed to the broadening of the horizons of education and its purpose in society. The Right Livelihood Foundation exists to promote 'a search for self-realisation and the realisation of values'. In this way the Foundation has tried to promote and support a process of informed educational debate and practice which will help to transcend the critical problems confronting people in the closing decades of the twentieth century.

The Wrekin Trust was formed in 1971 by Sir George Trevelyan, who was, for twenty years, the Principal of Attingham Park, the Shropshire Adult Education College. During this period he mounted a series of conferences on various aspects of spiritual knowledge, bringing together thousands of people whose convictions emanated from an awareness of spiritual values, and who were concerned about the prevailing climate of materialism. The name comes from the Wrekin, a mountain in Shropshire in the English Midlands. The work of the Trust is to educate people towards an awareness of a holistic and spiritual world view. "The work of the Wrekin Trust is not tied to any dogmas or religions. We do not need any new religions today, but we do need religion in the original sense of the word. Religare- to re-connect ourselves with our source and with our world, to understand that the needs of the person and the needs of the planet are today the same, and to live accordingly". (1)

Trevelyan's approach to education, "recognises that ideas are alive. In a Platonic sense they are truly Beings from the Ocean of Divine thinking and are fulfilled when they can operate in human thinking. They are dynamic and call for a change in life style . . . Living ideas result in a fundamental shift in our consciousness and therefore our action." (2)

The Trust promotes courses whereby participants can develop an understanding of a holistic world view, where the earth is viewed as a living creature, of which man is an integral part. It has promoted conferences on Holistic Healing, bringing together mystics and scientists and helping to overcome the separation between them. Trevelyan sees a general spiritual awakening as part of the emergence of a movement for a New Age, concerned with practical experiments in an alternative life style: "We are watching the emergence and linking of cooperative community ventures concerned with the Alternative Life-style. These may include organic husbandry for the growing and marketing of whole food, the opening of craft centres, alternative technology, new schools, and centres for meditation, healing and yoga. The wide movement for conservation of our countryside, planting of trees and animal welfare must be included. It is not necessary for those concerned with conservation to subscribe fully to the spiritual world-view, but we may see that they are truly serving the Earth as stewards of her life'. (3)

The work of Patrick van Rensburg has combined the representation of human rights with the quest for educational and cultural change, in an eminently practical fashion. Van Rensburg resigned his post as South African Vice-Consul in Leopoldville, Belgian Congo, in 1957. He subsequently became the organising secretary of the Liberal Party of South Africa, based in the Transvaal. While in Britain in 1959 he became involved in the campaign to boycott South African goods, and helped to launch the Boycott Movement, the forerunner of the Anti-Apartheid Movement. He was forced to flee South Africa during the State of Emergency which followed the Sharpville shootings. He went to Bechuanaland in 1962, where he founded Swaneng Hill School and the Brigade Movement, geared to the formation of producers' cooperatives. He later founded the Shashe River School in Botswana, and from the 1970s he has concentrated on the Brigades movement, on rural development, and on the continued development of secondary school reforms. Much of his current work is carried out through the Foundation for Education with Production in Botswana. His philosophy is described in his speech in this section, and it echoes and reinforces many of the projects whose work have been recognised since 1980 for the Right Livelihood Award. In van Rensburg's words: "Education would be a vast cooperative effort of everyone in society, and it would not be divorced from work and production'. His approach envisaged a "new total conception (of) permanent learning environments in conjunction with production and a variety of communally organised services and facilities for recreation, sport and cultural pursuits. Research should be functional and related to the real work and lives of communities, involving as many people, of all ages, as possible." (4)

NOTES:

1. Jakob von Uexkull, Introductory Speech, 1982.
2. Sir George Trevelyan, Statement on the Wrekin Trust, 1982.
3. Ibid.
4. Patrick van Rensburg.

HUMAN RIGHTS

Theodoor van Boven

9th December, 1985

LET ME first of all, also on behalf of my wife who shares this honour with me, express my gratitude to the Right Livelihood Foundation for inviting us to come to Stockholm in order to receive the Honorary Award for 1985. When the news of my selection reached us, this came as a complete and welcome surprise. Having been involved during a large part of my life in efforts to promote human rights, I am very honoured that these efforts have been recognized as in line with the very motives which inspired the creation of the Right Livelihood Foundation. As Jakob von Uexkull, the original sponsor of the Foundation stated: "Right Livelihood is to 'live lightly' on the earth entrusted to us, not to use more than our fair share of its resources. It is a call to everyone of us to take personal responsibility for the consequences of our actions on the world and to create a society in which that is practically possible".

These ideas of a fair share, of personal responsibility, of respect for fellow human beings and for the natural and living environment, are also basic human rights notions. The same ideas find expression in the Charter of the United Nations, in the Universal Declaration of Human Rights, and in numerous United Nations documents which seek to promote peace and justice. The United Nations Charter does not project human rights in a narrow and isolated context, but in a mutual relationship with the maintenance of international peace and security and the promotion of economic and social cooperation and development. Peace, development, and human rights are essentially inter-related, inter-dependent and indivisible.

At this august occasion I will share some thoughts with you and dwell on two issues which will, I hope, attract your attention, viz, (i) the threats to survival and (ii) the third system.

The Threats To Survival.

Right Livelihood is a way of life and vocation. Right Livelihood also means accepting and sharing responsibility for the preservation of life on this planet. Humankind as a whole is facing in an unprecedented and dramatic manner the hazards of total destruction. Forty years ago, a few months after the signing of the United Nations Charter in San Fransisco, the explosion of atomic bombs over Japan, with their immensely devastating effects, demonstrated the terrible and fatal dimensions of the atomic age. Today, strategies are being designed for the militarization of outer space and we are being warned that we find ourselves at the edge of perhaps the most far-reaching military threshold since the beginning of the atomic age. Precious as the notions of peace and justice may be, and will be, the keyword now is the very basic notion of survival.

It sometimes occurs to me to wonder—and the reference in the preamble of the United Nations Charter have led me to this thought—how future generations succeeding us (if there will be any) will judge our lifetime, our livelihood, our policies and priorities and the way we acted as stewards of the world's human, natural and other resources. If there will be human survival and if objective conditions would exist to reach an overall judgement of the predominant policies and priorities of our times, the verdict by future generations cannot but be harsh. How can it be explained and justified, under any standards of justice, that huge and ever increasing amounts of resources be allocated to the production of the most destructive conventional and nuclear arms, while at the same time some four billion people are lacking the most basic needs and struggling daily for their survival. Although it would be too simplistic to assume that everything that could be saved by limiting military expenditure could easily be diverted into development efforts, there is nevertheless such an enormous disproportion as regards allocations of resources aimed at meeting basic human needs, in comparison with resources directed at what are supposedly military security interests, that this situation is bound to be judged as a scandal by present and future generations.

In international relations, and within many societies, the philosophy of survival of the fittest, (which is essentially an anti-human rights notion), and the dictates of the strongest, are prevailing over the demands of peace and justice for all. The arms race and the aims of development have to be approached in their mutual and competitive relationship. While the frantic race towards nuclear conflagration, and the imminent spread of nuclear weapons among nations, poses a grave threat to the survival of humankind, this should not obscure the fact that for many millions the most immediate threat to survival is posed by various local, national and international conflicts which rage around the world, and by the lack of the most basic needs of existence.

I am quite aware that the laws of morality count very little for those who defend the laws of force. But I am also convinced that the laws of force, which are at the basis of patterns of domination and policies of deterrence are, apart from being morally condemnable and ethically unjust, not capable of safeguarding peace and security in the long run. There are eminent scientists who, in good conscience and in a spirit of right livelihood, put to themselves and to the world pertinent questions about the implications of their research for humanity and for the natural and biological environment. These questions touch upon issues of fundamental existence and survival. There are leading economists who, also guided by a sense of responsibility and by profound notions of right livelihood, are questioning the priorities which are dictated by rampant militarism and by the uncontrolled demands of the military-industrial complex. They have offered schemes for the conversion of military expenditure to civilian production, which would serve the rights and interests of the peoples of both developed and developing countries. There are conscientious lawyers who seek to give normative content to rights to development as foundations for a new social and human order at national and international levels. In this respect it may be recalled that a body of legal experts from all parts of the world, entrusted in the framework of the United Nations with the implementation of the International Covenant on Civil and Political Rights, adopted about a year ago (by consensus, in connection with its interpretative comments on the right to life) the following statement: "The production, testing, possession, deployment and use of nuclear weapons should be prohibited and recognized as crimes against humanity". Lawyers, philosophers and theologians have in the past developed doctrines of a 'just war', a concept often abused and now largely written off as legally unacceptable, and to be substituted by the concept of a 'just peace'. New emphasis and a new orientation is being directed at what a 'just peace' means and what it requires. It is definitely not the peace of a graveyard.

The Third System.

It would be erroneous if the global and structural issues facing us today would lead us to abandon our responsibilities as individual human beings, so as to indulge ourselves in an attitude of 'laisser faire, laisser aller'. It would assume that the management of the welfare and interests of humankind could suitably be left to institutions and mechanisms which are controlled by the established political and economic powers. I for one am not confident that the major powers which dominate national and international society are always mindful of the best interests of the people. In fact, a wealth of arguments and examples can be adduced to corroborate this view. The second reason why we cannot afford to be ruled out as responsible human beings is that, in spite of global and structural conditions which affect the community of nations and large sectors of humankind, work on the grass roots level does count and does have an impact on relationships between human beings, and may constitute a sign of hope and encouragement.

It is from this perspective that we see evolving what by the International Foundation for Development Alternatives (IFDA) has been aptly denominated as "the third system". This system is of a different nature than the first and second systems, which are constituted respectively by the inter-state and inter-governmental structures, and by a network of transnational corporations. The first and second systems represent political, economic and military powers and often go hand in hand. The third system is envisaged to serve the rights and interests of individuals and peoples, in particular the underprivileged, the deprived, the persecuted, the people having no voice. The third system could also be seen as a system of right livelihood, as a system of solidarity and concern that takes at heart the common standards of achievement enshrined in the Universal Declaration of Human Rights, and in other documents of the United Nations, setting out principles and programmes for a new human and social order at national and international levels. In the third system we find groups and organizations that defend the human factor, and advocate a people's oriented approach instead of relying on domination by power, strategies of deterrence, and the laws of force. This system has no fixed structure, but can be considered as a broad movement emanating from the grass roots of society. It comprises among others, religious workers, trade union peoples, workers in the field of education and development, and all those who are active in promoting and defending the rights of the deprived, and who work for their liberation and self-determination and for a more just society. Peace movements, environmental activists and numerous groups and organizations that expose violations of human rights belong to this movement, as well as women's organizations and defenders of the rights of minorities and of indigenous populations.

Having worked for a considerable period of my life with the United Nations, which is predominantly an inter-governmental system of cooperation, I have always considered the non-governmental organizations and private groups as indispensable partners of the World Organization, for the proper carrying out of its responsibilities. I have always tried to open up channels of communication between the United Nations and these non-governmental partners in order to maximize the impact of the peoples' interests. This was of course not always appreciated by governmental circles. These experiences convinced me very strongly that all efforts are needed to strengthen what we call the third system. In recent years, after my departure for the United Nations, I got involved in some of these efforts, which I will mention very briefly, in order to illustrate the operation of the third system. Thus, the European Human Rights Foundation is supporting, through modest grants, a large number of specific human rights projects and actions, preferably of an innovative nature and with impact on the grass roots, in many parts of the world. International Alert, a Standing International Forum of Group Conflict, Development and Human Rights, seeks to draw attention to problems of group conflict which seriously affects human rights; which inhibit development and result in mass killings and even genocide; and aims to focus on such emergency situations as are prevailing in Sri Lanka and Uganda. The International

Defence and Aid Fund for Southern Africa has as its primary objectives to provide aid for the legal defence of victims of unjust legislation and oppressive and arbitrary procedures in South Africa and Namibia, as well as to support their families and dependants. The International Commission of Humanitarian Inquiry into the conditions of displaced persons in Afghanistan identifies and assesses the needs of people lacking the assistance of the official inter-governmental community, and relying for their survival on humanitarian aid by non-governmental agencies and groups.

All these efforts, which serve as examples and illustrations of the many ways in which the third system operates, have in common that they seek to strengthen, to substitute or to redress where official systems of government, administration and protection are inadequate, deficient or unjust. In many instances it is crucial that, as a first step and for the sake of raising awareness and concern, barriers of silence be broken, patterns of injustice be identified and facts become known about the affected people. In this respect the role of the media and of investigative journalism can hardly be overestimated. However, the third system should not solely consist of crying voices in the wilderness—important as such voices may be—but also develop mechanisms of pressure, influence and cooperation with organizations and intitutions that may exercise leverage. The third system cannot operate effectively by remaining totally aloof as regards the power interests embodied in the first and second systems. The International Foundation for Development Alternatives (IFDA) elaborated a few years ago, on the basis of its "Third System Project", a blueprint for mechanisms of implementation which I consider very helpful and realistic. Central in this scheme is the notion of accountability and the establishment of mechanisms to enforce accountability. It was stated by IFDA: "The principle of accountability is an expansion of the rights of human beings, as individuals (human rights) and as societies (peoples' rights). It is an active concept. It calls for citizens to challenge, with courage and militancy, a power structure alienated from them. It is an instrument of democracy".

Much more could be and was said on this score, but let us retain for present purposes that the methods of critical dialogue and challenge are key elements in the relationships of the third system with the established powers.

There are at present strong ideological currents and powerful governmental policies that move away from multilateral cooperation, and consider the United Nations irrelevant, or, at best, of marginal importance. I wish to stress that from the perspective of the third system the United Nations, in spite of its serious shortcomings, carries great potentialities and deserves our strong support. In this respect I may highlight two factors which make the United Nations of crucial importance for devising and implementing third system strategies. First and foremost, we should never overlook that the United Nations has elaborated over the years a large body of international standards, as well as programmes for international action and cooperation, in such areas as human rights, the elimination of racial and sexual discrimination, arms control and disarmament, environment development, the habitat, population and in many other fields affecting the human condition.

The third system may also use the United Nations in another way, both for its own benefit and for the benefit of the World Organization. It can make, through the United Nations, an input and an impact by launching ideas, by making suggestions and proposals, by transmitting information, by expressing concerns and, as the case may be, by activities of exposure. The United Nations provides, also for the non-governmental sector, a platform and channel of communication as well as a forum of cooperation and dialogue.

THE RIGHTS OF PRISONERS

Winefreda Estanero-Geonzon (on behalf of Free Lava)

9th December 1984

I REPRESENT an umbrella organization of twenty eight community based groups, known as the Free Lava or The Free Legal Assistance Volunteers Association which is based in the City of Cebu, the largest city outside Manila, Philippines. The Free Lava is a service organization registered under the laws of our country. We are a non-political and a non-religious group. We advocate a three-angled programme of legal aid, namely: crime prevention, free legal assistance, and rehabilitation.

Our government has its own Citizens Legal Assistance Office (CLAO) which caters for the needs of poor litigants, with offices throughout the land. The association of lawyers, the Integrated Bar of The Philippines, also has its own legal aid office run as a public service, with chapters throughout the country. Free Lava is a private organisation which has been organised out of the need to meet certain conditions prevailing in our country.

Our civilian courts have functioned normally despite the imposition of martial law in 1972. However, there were certain types of cases, involving the security of the state, that were tried by the military tribunal. In 1981, martial law was lifted and all cases were tried by civilian courts, except those involving the members of the military and the police force. These are now subject to the military tribunal.

In the later part of 1978, I was appointed as the legal aid director of the Cebu City Chapter of the Integrated Bar of the Philippines. At that time, martial law was still operating. As legal aid director I visited many jails. I knew that there were, and still are, prisoners languishing in jail without trial and without access to advice. Despite the existence of government legal aid offices, I discovered the following abuses in our jails:

a) prisoners who were in jail for almost five years, without charges.

b) prisoners whose existence was not known to the courts, despite their long stay in jail.

c) prisoners who had been charged twice with the same offence.

d) prisoners who could have been released a long time ago, had their cases been tried on time.

e) very young children mixed up with adult and hardened criminals.

f) prisoners who attempted to kill themselves for loss of hope.

I decided to concentrate on the following types of case:

a) prisoners who could not afford to hire the services of counsel.

b) victims of violations of human rights, no matter by whom they are committed.

c) urban poor or slum dwellers, in their struggle for social justice.

In March, 1979, I met thirty nine minors in the Cebu City jail who would have served their sentence, had their cases come to court. In our country, we have a Presidential Decree, called PD 603, which calls for the suspension of the promulgation of the sentence of a minor found guilty. Instead he is given a chance to reform, and placed in a rehabilitation centre. On one occasion I met thirty nine such people who were given very minor penalties, but who were kept in jail far beyond their sentence of conviction. More than ten of them were given a sentence of reprimand or public censure (which does not need imprisonment), yet they were imprisoned for almost three years.

As there were no rehabilitation activities in jail, and in order to save the future of the minors, I organized a boy scout movement to enable them to get certificates of good behaviour. I have been connected with the boy scout movement in our country for the last 22 years, and I find it to be very fitted to the boys.

One by one, they were released and their cases were dismissed. At the same time we asked the assistance of the church, and other concerned persons in our community, to help us meet the basic needs of the prisoners.There were many who had no mats to sleep on; many sleep on bare cement floors with no shirts on, for lack of adequate clothing. We could not just close our eyes to the overcrowded cells, with very poor ventilation. In fact, the cells smelt of foul urine and sweat, and it was nauseating to go from one cell to another to interview prisoners who were beckoning to us. With many persons and clubs offering to assist, we formally organized the Civic Assistance Team to take care of the prisoners' basic needs.

Because I did boy scout and social work activities in jail, I was criticized by some of my colleagues for activities which were far from my position as the chapter's legal aid officer. My president told me to concentrate on purely legal work and leave the social work to the Ministry of Social Services and Development, an agency of the government. However, we could not wait until this office would do its task. We saw a wastage of human energy in jail— men and women with nothing to do except eat, stand, sit, walk and stare at blank walls every day, waiting for their deliverance from bondage.

Since I was restricted in this way, I sought the help of women lawyers, and brought to their attention the plight of prisoners in our jails, the immediate assistance that they needed, and the conditions they were in. The women lawyers responded. Hence, I continued my work in the name of the Association of Lawyers in Cebu, locally known as the FIDA or the Federacion Internacional de Abogadas. We also asked the help of local educational institutions and other clubs to provide rehabilitation activites, (handicraft making, literacy classes, farming, printing, and others).

As time went on, I could not cope with the growing number of cases referred to me regarding abuses by some men in the military, as well as the cases of prisoners in jail. I sought the help of other lawyers who were willing to help, but on the condition that they need not visit the jail. They would only appear in the courts. Hence, I sought the assistance of local universities to provide legal aid volunteers. Many law students, political science students and social work interns responded. To make them effective, we conducted para-legal seminars and trained them to make follow ups. We organized aid volunteers from among the community based groups which meet regularly. Thus, we formed three services, namely the Documentation and Research Group; the Legal Services Group; and the Civic Assistance Group. With twenty three community based organizations working hand in hand, we organized the Free Lava; and this was still under the umbrella of Cebu City Chapter of the Integrated Bar of the Philippines.

The linkages we have with the community based groups in the Lava organisation drew attention from other countries in Asia. We had visitors from Papua New Guinea, Thailand, Taiwan, Malaysia, Indonesia and also from the United States.

In 1981 martial law was lifted. Despite this we have some policemen and soldiers in our area who have a martial law mentality, and who believe that the military is supreme. Consequently our office has been flooded with requests for assistance to help the victims of abuses by men in uniform.

We met prisoners who still suffer from the agonies of maltreatment, either committed during their arrests or during custodial interrogations. As we listened to the agonies of the victims, to the cries of the widows and orphans, we became angry too, and sometimes we felt we were fighting the mighty Goliath with a toothpick.

Believing in the inherent goodness of man, and strongly believing that maltreatment and abuses are not mandated or directed from above, we sought a series of dialogues with the top ranking officials of the military. Across the conference tables with the highest military official in our region, the regional commander and his station commanders, we presented the abuses committed by some of their men in the lower ranks. We brought with us the living victims of the abuses; we brought pictures along for those who could not come; we presented documents. In dialogues, we made the military understand the need to provide a forum of justice to the victims of abuses, and the dangers our society would be in if grievances are not attended to. We know that when a person is desperate, he knows no law. We want to live in an atmosphere of love and brotherhood. The top ranking officials understood our viewpoint. Two days after the dialogue, the newspapers carried in their headlines a presidential order to oust bad elements and undesirables from the military service. Hence, we encourage our people to come out, and not to be afraid, to denounce abuses of all kinds, as we are willing to give our legal services free.

Later, I felt a vacuum within me. I felt that something is lacking in what I do. While I help victims of injustice, how about the criminally inclined? While we free the body from bondage, how about the soul?

Hence, in addition to what we have been doing, we inject rehabilitation through spiritual means, in addition to the existing civic assistance programs (like handicraft, farming, pig raising, literacy classes and boy scouting, and so on).

I formally organized the Prison Ministry of the

Charismatic of Renewal, the biggest movement now going on in our country. I introduced the concept that prison work is not only confined to jail centers, but should also include activities to minimize the number of people in jail.

Hence, as part of the crime prevention programme, we organize the poorest in our society, the slum dwellers, the vendors, the farmers, the labourers, and the homeless. We conduct seminars on human rights for them. We organize legal aid volunteers from among them, and meet them regularly. We make them see that they could turn to us for help if they are abused and harassed. We bring their grievances to the authorities.

For our clients in jail, we regularly conduct spiritual and social activities. We trace back the reasons why they are in jail. Is it because of economic necessity? Is it because they are victims of mistaken identity; of malicious prosecution to make it appear that crimes are solved? Are they criminally inclined? Is he a drug addict because of his desire to seek happiness which his parents could not give? In our work, we discover that many prisoners are products of broken homes. Hence, we conduct dialogues with the parents.

Because these activities are far from my job as a lawyer in a legal aid office, I resigned from my post and registered the Free Lava, doing separate but coordinated services related to crime prevention, legal assistance, and rehabilitation. We organize our clients in jail, and help them have a governing body composed of rehabilitated inmates. With the approval of the jail management, the leaders council is now given a voice to police and supervise their own ranks. As we could not do anything about separating children from adults, (because of the absence of a separate detention home), we trained the members of the council as scoutmasters. Thus we have in Cebu the only boy scout movement where the adult prisoners are scoutmasters for the minor boy scouts, who are also in the prison. We follow up released prisoners with the help of volunteer workers. We assist them to get small business loans (equivalent to $15 or $20 US dollars), payable in instalments to start with. We know that the hardest thing for a released prisoner to do is to get a job. We now are intensifying the organization of community scout troops of thirty two young boys in the squatter areas. The idea is to give them income generating projects, for the greatest enemies we have are crimes against property brought about by poverty.

The time given to me is too short to enumerate in detail the activities of the Free Lava. There are many other things that we do. Let me mention in passing that in our work we find it futile to criticize without offering alternatives. We find it useless to curse the dark. It is always better to light a candle. We have proven countless times that man is by nature good. In our work we see the beauty of reconciliation, rather than direct confrontation.

GRASSROOTS DEVELOPMENT

Rajni Kothari (on behalf of LOKAYAN)

9th December 1985

LOKAYAN believes in intervening in the social process through the method of dialogue, and its concomitant processes. It seeks to provide a broad platform of debate, documenting reality on diverse issues, undertaking research arising out of the felt need of activists, and disseminating all this widely among both activists and the public at large. It believes in the primacy of dialogue because of its perception that we live in a deeply divided world with increasing loss of contact and growing estrangement between people. It is an estrangement that not only promotes ignorance and loss of empathy, but, through capsuled stereotypes and in-built prejudices, creates a psychic condition of growing immunization, apathy and amnesia. We live in a habitat consisting of two worlds that are so wide apart that it is just not possible to think of them as being one. This is not along the post-war stereotypes of the capitalist and communist worlds, or the North and the South, or the earlier one of the West versus the East. The two worlds I speak of cut across all these, along the simple indicators of human survival and access to resources and life opportunitites, as well as access to political power and decision-making institutions.

The "two worlds" are also found within each nation and at the lower reaches of territorial existence. Thus there are not just two worlds inhabiting this planet of ours, but also two

Indias; and within India, each political entity and each human settlement, whether urban or rural, is split into two. This split undermines both larger unities of the national or the subregional kind, and the sense of community at the local level. But, even worse than this, there is another process at work which undermines the rich social diversity and cultural plurality through which a sense of unity had been organically felt for so long. Modern technology, and the modern State, seek to deal with the problem of poverty (or exploitation, or inequity) by imposing centralizing and homogenizing solutions that are meant to "integrate" various elements. But in fact modern economy and the modern State destroy natural and cultural diversity and, far from integrating, in fact, produce a basically dualist economy and centralising State. The modern project of integration, whether into the world economic market or into the world strategic order and the technological marketplace, has effectively split each society into two. And the more the integration of the one segment, the less the care and understanding and knowledge about the other.

The Lokayan dialogues are a way of raising issues that go to the heart of the great divide between the two Indias. We do this in a variety of ways; for example, through contact and communication between academics, professionals and opinion-makers residing in the metropolitan world, and activists and political cadres working among groups and constituencies in the non-metropolitan, "vernacular" world. Another method is through dialogue among individuals sensitized to the grassroots reality in different ways, or having different ideological interpretations of that reality. And, above all, through establishing contact and building relationships among the activists themselves, and through them the diverse public they attempt to serve. We have found that the world of action, too, is a highly divided world. So is the world of knowledge, social analysis, and ideological interpretation.

Lokayan is an attempt to build bridges across both the world of action and the world of knowledge. It is also an attempt at normative interventions—we seek to do all this simultaneously, and not in separate compartments of reflection and action, theory and praxis, science and practical knowledge. In this lies Lokayan's distinctiveness as a method of social intervention: relating and interrelating diverse segments of practical reality, and enabling the practitioners of knowledge to participate in the building of the same interrelationships.

Lokayan also represents a mode of action, of intervention, of politics, of struggle. While its members operate outside the Parliamentary and the party spaces, their work and activities, including the knowledge and intellectual debate they generate, are clearly political in nature. It is just that these are carried out in different parts of the political process, through quite different infrastructures of democratic participation from those in which political parties and electoral machines operate. In articulating this process, Lokayan activists employ forms and procedures of intellectual intervention in ways that assist and enhance the political role of action groups and individuals engaged in political acts. There is an impression about Lokayan that it consists of a bunch of intellectuals who meet and talk, write and publish—that it is not concerned with action. This is not true. Lokayan's innovation is to closely relate its activities to the concerns and problems of those involved in political action, from the grassroots to the national—and in some ways international—thresholds. On the other hand, Lokayan operates from a basic premise arising out of its perception and understanding of the crisis of our times; that it is fundamentally an intellectual crisis, a crisis of ideas, a crisis of human knowledge, both generally, but also especially in the social arena. The stock of theories and models of social change which have shaped modern industrial civilization, its colonial expansion, and its subsequent even larger expansion through the paradigm of modernization and development, has created the world we live in. It is a world in an undesirable state in numerous ways, particularly because of the intellectual tutelage of the whole world to post-Enlightenment Western models, and to the framework of modern science and technology, (through which these models have structured patterns of domination, manipulation and violence). This undesirable state of affairs cannot be substantially changed without raising basic questions about the structure of economic and political reality, and the ideas and assumptions underlying it. We must also come forward with alternative answers to existing ways of managing the world. This is fundamentally an intellectual task, and an intellectual-political task. This is our conviction.

It is in the manner of conceiving and pursuing this intellectual-political task that Lokayan's specificity and methodology has developed. Lokayan has been a movement away from specialized knowledge, to what we call social knowledge. While it promotes carefully conducted studies in selected problem areas, it has moved away from the cool and amoral conception of scientific objecivity, which does not permit one to take sides. We believe in taking sides, not in any dogmatic or sectarian manner, or in any watertight ideological frame, but on the basis of informed dialogue between diverse or opposing points of view. Lokayan conceives of the knowledge process as one of participation and involvement of diverse people, not only of academics and intellectuals but also of activists, professionals and politicians. Indeed, Lokayan's basic input into India's intellectual, political and social life has been that based on activist—intellectual interactions which are raising new issues, asking questions and redefining the agenda of both political action and political theory.

The activity of raising new questions and coming up with new issues does not take place in a vacuum. Nor is there some previously well thought out grand design that only ideologues and model-builders are given to indulge in. Our thinking has gradually crystallized from a series of interactions between different strands. It has arisen out of struggles against existing hegemonies in the social structure; from resistance to exploitation and inequities generated by the development process; from new forms of protest within the broad civil liberties and human rights movement; and from new and alternative ideas and experiments in technology, social and economic organization, and modes of decision making and participation. Lokayan's is an effort to broaden the scope and the range of politics, to open up new spaces in both the sphere of the State, and in the large and complex terrain of civil society outside the State, which in India presetnts a vast arena. Lokayan is concerned with this simultaneous process of "conscientization", of engagement in actual struggles, as well as a search for new alternatives on a variety of concrete tasks.

The process has given rise to a new class of people drawn from the highly conscious and politicized stream of the middle classes. These individuals are engaged in a wide range of grassroots activism, but also in broad touch with the larger context within which their work among the distressed and the restless masses has to be carried out. This convergence of restless people becoming increasingly conscious of their plight, with a class of volunteer politicians on the one had and a group of concerned intellectuals on the other, has produced a new grassroots movement in India. Such a convergence of activists and intellectuals is gradually making it possible to articulate and present the large numbers and wide range of micro experiments and struggles in a macro perspective. This is precisely where Lokayan's overall aim and perspective lie—in bringing to bear, at the threshold of macro politics, the stirrings and struggles that have appeared in a variety of micro settings. It is a process still under way, and has by no means been fulfilled. But it has begun.

From this process another convergence is taking shape:

new definitions of the agenda of politics and the rise of new social movements. For example, the issue of the environment. It is something that can no longer be left to experts in ecology or in economic development, or to environmental departments. These departments may have been set up in response to popular pressures, but they have now become part of the bureaucratic status quo. Nor can environmental problems be left to be sorted out in the future. The environment must be preserved and regenerated here and now, and cannot be left to the pious declarations of governments. It must become part of people's own active involvement, and of agitation to restrain State and corporate interests from destroying the resource base of the poor, and of future generations. Equally, there must be concern for the resources of non-human species and plants with whom our lives are organically linked. Ordinary people understand this much more than experts.

The same is the case with health; with access and entitlement to food and nutrition; with shelter and housing. It is increasingly being realized that the new hazards to health, the new epidemics that are breaking out, and the problems associated with modern drugs, are in good part a product precisely of experts in the medical profession. The horrors let loose by chemical industries and nuclear plants are increasingly coming to light; the tragedy in Bhopal dramatised this, but it is happening in many other places too. Attempts at self-relience in food production (as in India) have little to do with actual access and entitlement to that food for the poor. The same applies to shelter and housing, and to the availability of drinking water and access to fuel. The green and the white "revolutions"; the revolution in materials technology, and the umpteen schemes of "Housing for the poor", have not been able to remove the scourge of hunger and malnutrition. Millions are without shelter; still more millions are being driven from the rural areas into ghettos of dirt, squalor and disease in the cities from where they are then bulldozed, driven away, and tossed around hither and thither. The poor have been reduced to being a stateless people in their own State. These things make matters, hitherto considered issues for experts and specialized handling, into urgent political tasks.

Implied in this is yet another change that has taken place in the thinking on development, and which has a bearing on practical politics and intellectual work. The earlier logic of development, based on accumulation-distribution—(in which distribution was to be taken care of at a later stage)— has been exposed and repudiated. Implied in that logic was another presumption, never fully spelt out. It looked upon people as objects, not as subjects in their own right; as beneficiaries of the process of development, not as direct participants in it. Thus, they had no control over how things should go. And things have gone awry. With this realization has also come the conviction that the process of distribution; of access and empowerment; of narrowing gaps and countering monopolies—these are matters in which the people themselves will have to be involved, through their own organizations, and through their own conceptions of what is relevant and what is not. These are issues of sheer survival; they are too serious to be left to either technocrats or professional politicians.

Nowhere is the enlargement and redefinition of the scope of politics brought out as vividly and dramatically as in what is called the women's movement. I prefer to think of it as a feminist input into our whole thinking on politics. It has not just enlarged the scope of politics by bringing into its ambit what was until recently considered a personal and private world. From the position that the personal and the political are polar opposites, to the one that claims the "personal is political", is a massive shift, not just in the position of women in politics, but in our whole understanding of politics as such.

The entry of women into politics is leading to new

approaches and methods to deal with basic problems like the environment, health, drunkenness, sanitation, and the reassertion of community needs in the choice of technology. The feminist input serves not just women, but men too. There is no limiting relationship between feminist values and being a woman. Above all, there is emerging an unprecedented convergence—between the ecological and feminist movements, and between these and the peace movement. This has already happened in Europe, with the spectacular spread of the peace movement and with the affirmation that peace and disarmament are too important to be left to governments. Women have played a major role in the realisation that, left to themselves, governments will in all likelihood blow up the world.

This is yet to happen in our part of the world. Our people are still under the spell of theories of threat from within and without. But the awakening will come here too, even if it takes time and calls for much greater effort to build pressures from the grassroots; we just cannot afford to be prisoners of this arms race, and women will have to play a major role in changing this.

The more important point is one about the interrelationahip of issues and movements, of a holistic approach to life, which goes against the grain of the modern scientific culture with its emphasis on specialization and fragmentation. As women come out of their presently narrow approach of catching up with men, and as feminist values become more generalised for humanity as a whole, a holistic approach will develop. It will be an approach that is also plural, and based on complementarities. This is more likely to happen in the non-Western world than in the West because our cultures have always been embedded in a holistic way of life; they have just been recessive in recent times.

Our efforts are by no means successful; all we can claim is that the voices which we express cannot any longer be suppressed. We do realize the larger context in which we operate. It is a context in which the engines of growth are in decline; where the organised working class is declining; where the process of marginalisation is spreading; where technology is turning anti-people; where development has become an instrument of the privileged class; and where the State has lost its role as an agent of transformation, or even as a protector and mediator in the affairs of the civil society. The whole relationship between the State and civil society is increasingly being visited by a growing coercion of the State apparatus. There is a growing demand for unity and consensus—not in the form of an organic expression of civil society, but in the form of compliance with whatever happens to be the ruling orthodoxy. As this happens, the State becomes more and more repressive.

All this is taking place within a global context in which the centralising thrust does not stop at the national centre; it makes the nation-state itself an abject onlooker and a client of a global 'world order'. It is a context of growing international pressures, and of subtle brainwashing which heralds the end of self-reliance in the developing countries. There is at work a process of integration of the organised national economy into the world market, while millions of people are removed from the economy. They have become impoverished, destitute, drained of their own resources, and deprived of the minimum requirements of health and nutrition. They are denied 'entitlement' to food, fuel, water and shelter, and even access to their traditional cultures. In short they have been made an unwanted and dispensible lot whose fate seems to be 'doomed'.

It is with the plight of these rejects of society and of organised politics, that the grassroots movements and non-party formations in India are concerned. They are a part of the democratic struggle at various levels, in a radically different social context from what was posited both by the incrementalists and the revolutionaries. They have sprung up at a point of history when both existing institutions, and the theoretical models on which they were based, have run their course. There is a search for new instruments of political action in the large vacuums in political space which are emerging because of the decline in the role of the State as an agent of transformation, and the virtual collapse of 'government' in large parts of rural India. The grassroots movements and non-party formations are based on deep stirrings of consciousness, on an awareness of crisis that can conceivably be turned into a catalyst of new opportunities. They need to be seen as a response to the incapacity of the State to hold its various constituents in a framework of positive action; its growing refusal (not just inability) to 'deliver the goods' when it comes to the needs of poor; and its increasingly repressive character. The repression is directed against vulnerable sections of the population, against activists working among them, and against intellectual dissidents. What these groups and organisations are doing is to open alternative political spaces outside the usual arena of party and government, though not outside the State. When the State and other vested interests mount a backlash, these organisations are called upon to play a further role of nurturing and providing protection to the victims of this backlash. Lokayan both joins in this effort, and sensitizes the wider public to the realities on the ground.

PEACE IN LEBANON

Iman Khalife

9th December 1984

I HAVE WITH me a book illustrating the capital of Lebanon, Beirut. Beirut before and after the war. Beirut, the city that refuses to die. The photographs in the book picture a beautiful city—a happy city—a city of peace. I would like to have had several copies of it to distribute to those who never knew Beirut except in terms of destruction and violence, and to show how it became the arena of an ugly war which has now lasted nine years.

During these nine years the world knew Beirut as a city full of fear and fury, synonymous with war and death. Beirut has always been the cultural nerve center of the Middle East, and remained so in spite of the war. It is a meeting point for ideas from all over the Arab world, and a spring-board for Western discoveries and innovations.

My generation and I did not enjoy Beirut as a city of light and peace. My father was born in South Lebanon, I was born in the capital, Beirut. I spent my childhood in an environment full of goodwill and love. However, since my awareness of the world, I have only known Beirut and my country Lebanon—north and south, east and west—in a never ending strife, for reasons I cannot comprehend.

I entered university at the beginning of the war, a girl from a middle class family, trying to escape the horrors around me by focussing on fields that would satisfy my personality, and help me reach my goal. At the university I used to look at a playground within the larger campus grounds where children innocently played, completely unaware of the violence surrounding them. I decided to major in Child Psychology, and since then I have lived in conflict; conflict between the innocence of the children I teach, and the continuous war surrounding me and them.

I saw them running away from fear to their own world of innocence, and back again; I saw their fathers and mothers rushing to the small playground to take their children away to safety, looking for peace and security; I saw the unconscious struggle these children lived through in a war torn country, trying to maintain their innocence in the face of horror, and the sound of guns, rockets and bombs.

I saw this scene repeating itself every day, and at night, in my mind, the roots of alarm began to take hold at the danger the future might be reserving for these children, forgetting, in my concern for them, my own fears for my own future.

The war robbed these children of their childhood, and it robbed others like myself the chance to plan for a future.

From these feeling and thoughts stemmed the idea of the '6th of May Peace March'—This was my call:

> Nine years of this war have elapsed and we have been considering all the solutions in vain, resigned in our shelters . . . eating, drinking . . . sleeping. Hasn't the time come to ask ourselves, where does this lead to?
>
> How long for?
>
> Are we going to let the tenth year of (civil) war destroy us?
>
> Are we afraid & what is left to be afraid of?
>
> Let us all go out and join our voices to the other silent voices so it may become a resounding scream.
>
> Let us go out. Men, Women and Children.

Let us walk out of our silence and scream in one
voice . . . No to the war — No to the 10th year.
You might say what for? And who will listen?
Let's try together and see . . . Isn't the trying worth
the effort?
Who did not lose during these bitter years, souls,
properties . . . liberties and nerves?
Do you still care if you lose this experience?
We won't lose it.
Haven't we heard, haven't we read about peoples'
revolutions throughout history?
Let us walk out of our fear, and march together asking
to stop our tragedy and comedy at the same time.
We don't want cannons and shellings,
We don't want a distorted country,
We don't want a displaced homeless people.

We want simply to live in peace.
We want to raise up our children
and save our brothers and sisters . . .
We want our families to remain whole.
Let us walk out of our isolation and join one another
and march on May 6th from the Barbir and Palace of
Justice to the Museum at 12 noon, where we will meet
our brothers and sisters everywhere . . . from far or
near.
For all those who still have a grain of conscience; a little
hope and attachment for the future.
Let us walk out of our tears and screams of pain
And hold together our only Slogan . . .

    No to the war
    No to the 10th year
    Yes to life.

I was not introducing an original thought—it was not a
new idea. But it was the cry of the 'silent majority' voiced

aloud by a people who had suffered and endured nine years of ugly war, and by a people who carried no arms to defend themselves but struggled to avoid death, violence and ruin in order to live, to build and to continue to be. We took Gandhi's motto: "that the way to defeat tyranny is by using the weapons of non-violence".

Many of the Lebanese left Lebanon in search of safety and peace but the moment they felt that some measure of security was attained, they returned to their country to rebuild, regardless of the fact that they did not know whether that peace was permanent or momentary.

Despite the war the people remained undefeated. I would like here to cite an example of a Lebanese businessman who gave a chance to thousands of young people to work with dignity and integrity by creating jobs to rebuild their country, and to others by giving them loans and grants to study and continue their education in Lebanon and abroad.

I give this as an example, to emphasize the spirit that embodies Lebanon. These positive elements for reconstruction would not have occurred in any other country in normal circumstances.

It was this spirit that responded to the call for the '6th of May Peace March.' The call for peace voiced the feelings of every single person who wanted to express their desire for the love for peace.

This call and its response took the world by surprise. It shook the international community. They had forgotten that there is a people in Lebanon–a people whose cry for peace was over-shadowed by the sound of guns—a people who form the silent majority, and who have been undermined by the minority.

A committee of twenty people was formed. Members of this committe had not known each other before, but their faith in hope for peace united them: "Peace with its silence has a louder ring and higher pitch than the war with its loud explosions."

The response to the call was so great, so tremendous, that the war itself was afraid of such a loud cry. The day before the peace march was to take place, the most violent outburst of fighting erupted.

The march was cancelled as it would have defeated its purpose, which was to stop the killing, not to have more victims. Since that time I have received continuously an appeal from the people of Lebanon, urging that the message for peace should continue. As an alternative to the peace march, which might have resulted in bloodshed, a petition is being passed around the country and over seventy thousand signatures have been obtained.

Our movement is still informal and spontaneous. It meets to keep our voices heard, and to find ways to erase the evil traces of war in the minds of the Lebanese people, particularly the children. We work under very difficult circumstances with little resources but we work, each in his own capacity, as Gandhi did, by "finding always something constructive and positive to do whenever his protest and demonstrations were not workable".

True peace is not only the silence of guns, the absence of violence or the end to the state of war. On this principle we act to pursue our goal. Centuries ago, Spinoza said 'Peace was not the absence of war but a disposition for benevolence, truth and justice.' This definition shows how much the individual can achieve in his daily life in the name of peace. The people of South Lebanon live under Israeli occupation, ostensibly to secure peace on Israel's northern borders, regardless of the measures taken. As a result, to be able to visit my family in South Lebanon, I have to obtain a pass and endure three days at an Israeli check point. But many others, much more unfortunate than myself, suffer greater misfortunes. There are those who are refugees in their own country; not allowed back to their own land, to work their land, to gain their livelihood or to bury their dead. The humiliation and cruelty they suffer at the hands of the occupiers when trying to cross to their own villages in their own homeland, is done in the name of peace. Other areas in Lebanon suffer from oppressors, who deny them their right to peace, but the soul of every Lebanese, whether in the South, under Israeli occupation, or in other areas under other oppressors threatening his liberty as an individual, there is a true longing for peace. I call on the world community to share with us and join us in our efforts to put an end to all occupation and oppression and help us to raise the voice of peace loud and clear. Let us have peace, security, a restoration of confidence in humanity and a better world. I would like to thank all the members of the Right Livelihood Foundation for the appreciation of the '6th of May Peace March' which rightfully belongs to the Lebanese Silent Majority and, therefore, this award goes to them.

SPIRITUAL EDUCATION

Sir George Trevelyan

8th December 1982

THE MORE I look at the age which we are in now, the more I feel that mankind has reached the threshold of a new step in consciousness. When we get beyond this time of turmoil and change, a new Renaissance will be upon us. It is with this concept that we are concerned in the Wrekin Trust, which is an adult education movement concerned with the spiritual nature of man. In the sixties when I began to experiment with weekend courses on the great spiritual themes, like the expansion of consciousness or 'Death: the great adventure', I found that we packed the house. There was an immense response, and I realised that there was an aspect of adult education which was simply not being met: a quest for meaning in life, a quest for something beyond the materialistic, separatist way of looking at life. After I retired in 1971, it was clear that this was the work to be done. I founded an educational charity, (calling it after our local mountain, the Wrekin), in order to put on courses on the new world view emerging. I was joined by my co-director, Malcolm Lazarus, in 1974, and for 11 years we have put on courses and conferences, over 450 in different parts of Britain.

What happens in history can best be understood if we realise that the events are really symptoms of evolving consciousness. Everything is in evolution, and the most important feature is the evolution of consciousness. The great turning points in history can really be seen as symptoms thereof. What is happening in our time is the experience of such a shift in human consciousness, a paradigm shift, a shift in world view, particularly in the West. The greatest of our scientists are now arriving at views which are almost identical to the world view of the ancient mystery traditions. This is an extraordinary phenomenon. The ancient wisdom, called sometimes the Hermetic wisdom, gave us a picture of life where the universe was Mind, a Divine source from which poured out an ocean of thought, of intelligence, of living ideas. The Universe is seen not as a mechanism but an affair of consciousness, as a great creative source from which the forms of Nature have been derived.

The next point in the Hermetic wisdom, the wisdom of the ancient mystery initiation temples, was the Law of Correspondence: as above so below, as within so without, and as in the macrocosm so in the microcosm. The universe works as a great oneness, in which the whole is reflected in every part. The wonderful invention of the hologram and holographic photography illustrates this. With the use of laser beams we can photograph an object three dimensionally. We then make an extraordinary discovery that when a holographic plate is dropped and smashed, every fragment of it contains the whole photograph three dimensionally: each one has the whole! Two well-known scientists, Professor David Bohm and Karl Pribram, who have spoken at our 'Mystics and Scientists' conferences, suggest that the whole world is a hologram and every human mind is a fragment of this whole, and the whole is reflected in the fragment, in all its harmony and oneness. But the Greeks knew this too. Above the mystery temple of Eleusis was carved 'Man know thy self and thou shalt know the universe'.

That remark can mean nothing to a rational materialistic intellect. It does not make sense. The rational intellect has reached only the point of experiencing separation. That is the mote of our age. You experience yourself as a separate entity among a mass of other separate entities and things. In no sense can you say, as the Orient says: 'That art thou, you are me.' You aren't me! You are all sitting there and I am sitting here, and this table is sitting there, and a tree is growing out there. We are all separate. That is where the intellect founded on the five senses, on the experience of the senses, has got us to. The result of that development of consciousness, of reaching this point of intellectual self-consciousness, has enabled us to analyse Nature, to dissect Nature, to control Nature, to conquer Nature, (which is a terrible phrase) and to build the remarkable technological culture that is now ours.

But we have lost a tremendous truth which the Egyptians knew, the Greeks knew, which was taught in the mystery schools, where the students had the great initiation experience called the temple sleep. The selected candidate was laid out in a sarcophagus and his self, his ego, his 'I', and his soul were withdrawn by the initiating priest, as was most of what is called the etheric body, the structure of vital forces which holds the particles of the body together. This was all withdrawn, and you lay as one dead for three and a half days. In that time your real Self and 'I' and your soul body, your emotional body, travelled in the spiritual world and experienced directly that the 'I' in you is an imperishable droplet or spark of the Divine creative source. This cannot die even if the body is smashed or drowned or burned. After three and a half days, you were called back by the initiating priest who knew how to do the trick. You came alive again, sat up and climbed out of the coffin. But you remembered the spiritual world through which you had been travelling. You knew that in you is a deathless imperishable droplet of the Divine source, and you were filled with courage and joy to face the ordeals of life.

That knowledge was given directly to those ready for initiation. To the others it was taught by mythology, by myths and legends and dramas which told the great truths about the human soul and its development, and which appealed directly to the subconsciousness. In the evolution of consciousness we lost this vision, this Hermetic wisdom. We lost the key to the vision that we are beings of spirit, soul and body. There is an actual watershed moment when this happened. At the Church Council of Constantinople in 869, they decreed that it was now heresy for Christians to speak of man as spirit, soul and body. From now on he was to be considered as nothing but a body with a soul, having some spiritual qualities. That decision was a symptom of the changing consciousness: no longer could they grasp the true spiritual nature of the 'I' in man, of the Being in man. But as soon as you say that man is nothing but a body with a soul, it opens the door to thinking that the soul only begins at conception. You begin to doubt that it has any eternal qualities. You lose the sense that we are imperishable in our inner core or kernel, an imperishable droplet of Divinity.

The door was opened to the still greater depths of materialistic thinking. Dialectical materialism says that we are nothing but matter, only body. But this body is seen as having certain subtle qualities of a rather soul like nature. So in Russia they can study scientifically the most remarkable effects in the human aura and the subtle vibrations of the body without admitting to the existence of either soul or spirit! But now great scientists (physicists and brain specialists) are discovering that the universe is Mind, that everything is thought! They are rediscovering what the ancient wisdom and the mystical traditions have always known: that the universe is a great Oneness, that life works as a stupendous whole in an immense harmony, a unity though not a uniformity. Scientists are now saying that the earth is, in a true sense, a living creature with its own breathing and blood stream, its own intelligence, glands and sensitivity, and that the human being is not separate from nature but is that point where Nature has become self-conscious.

We are discovering what is called the holistic world view. This wonderful word had come into common use in the last five years. It implies the conviction that the whole is holy. There is no separation, everything is Divine. The great ocean of life and thought permeates everything. We are in it now in this room. We are 150 different personalities and bodies, but on a deeper level we are one mind, and that mind is a pulse of the eternal mind. The mystery traditions taught that the mind is the thinking of the great source, that, from mind, form has been produced; and that the convolutions of the human brain reflect the convolutions of cosmic thought. This globe within the head reflects the whole cosmos. The mystery traditions said it, and now great scientists are using precisely the same language. Science and mysticism come together again.

There is nothing wrong with our intellectual materialism. Our materialistic view is a phase which we in the West have to go through. We had to focus intelligence and intellect into the world of matter, and master matter. I do not believe it was a blunder or mistake. Man as a spiritual being chose to use his intellect to render matter into its smallest condition and master it. The price we had to pay was the loss of vision of the subtler worlds of being and spirit. The spiritual world simply disappeared. We could see nothing in nature other than the outward form. The subtler inner beings of nature became invisible to us. But in that process we have achieved human freedom by being detached from the Divine World. The question now is if we can learn to creatively handle that freedom and work with the ocean of creative life.

My theme is the New Renaissance. What was the first Renaissance? It is not enough to say that man discovered himself and the world. Seen on the deeper level, in the descent of the being of man (the thing that can say 'I' to itself) there came a moment when that descent was virtually complete. This was at the beginning of the 15th century. There was a physical, psychological, spiritual process in which the "I" of man came down and identified with the five senses. Our ancestors said: "Look at the beauty of my body and of nature! Let us start experimenting and exploring! Let us paint the body!" The result was a burst of creativity and of egoism. One of the notable things about the Renaissance is the inflation of the ego and the delight in colour, wealth and royalty. In this process of discovering the world and experiencing it, man lost himself as a spiritual being, lost his knowledge of his true nature. For centuries he plunged into the exploration of matter, and did wonderful things, but lost the purpose of life upon earth.

It is interesting that at the begining of the Renaissance we have this outburst of religious painting, as if the spiritual worlds were making an affirmation about the real nature of man. Man is a Divine being, and the body, as the Greeks knew, is the temple into which that divinity can descend. We have gone through the epoch of descent and we are in the process of coming up again. Our great poet prophet, William Blake, described it as the passage from innocence through experience to imagination. Out of Eden's garden we are drawn down through the fall, deeper and deeper to identification with the body and the five senses. Now we have the possibility to rise again, not back to Eden, but on to what is called the New Jerusalem. Or we can choose to go on downwards into a new bestiality lower than the animals. These are the horrors of our time: the great intellect with a powerful will and no heart, the torturers and tyrants of our age who are rejecting the possibility of the re-ascent.

We have analysed with our intellect the depths of matter, and discovered it is all energy. We have discovered that life is a great oneness, in perpetual movement. We have also discovered that we can release the energy within the nuclear centre, and taken upon ourself the god-like responsibility. We have to take full responsibility for our discoveries. We are now at the threshold. The first Renaissance moved down across a threshold into the world of the the senses. We are now beginning to move towards self-consciousness, into Divine mind. We can move our intellect into the universal intellect. They tell us we are using only 5% of our brain cells. What will happen when we use 20%, 40%, 60% of our cells? There is no limit to cosmic man as he extends his consciousness. Furthermore, he is opening himself once more to the working of the ocean of living archetypal ideas. We have to grasp the notion of a higher intelligence, on a higher frequency rate from which the forms of Nature have been deposited and formed. The world of living ideas can reflect in human thinking. We are opening once more to blend with the cosmic ocean of intelligence, and allow those ideas to come alight in our own creative thought. If the energy released in the 15th century, through the psychological change of man stepping down into the five senses, produced that astonishing burst of creativity we call the Renaissance, then what is going to happen when we do the reverse process—and move across that frontier and open up ourselves to working co-operatively with the world of creative ideas? There may start a Renaisssance beyond our wildest dreams.

EDUCATION FOR SOCIAL CHANGE

Patrick van Rensburg

9th December 1981

I WOULD like to thank Jakob von Uexkull and the Right Livelihood Foundation for this award to me.

The note on the presentation of this prize to me makes reference to the fact that I am a South African exile. Behind that story there was for me a long and painful process. I'm sure not many of you know what it means to be born into a society which inverts all values and stands them on their head, which brings you up to believe in the superiority of one race over another, which brings you up warning you that after a certain age you do not play with black children, Indian children or coloured children. You are born into that society and the way it brings you up leaves you with little choice.

I was born into a very ordinary South African family that believed in the virtue of racism. How do you disengage from that? You live in schools and in a society in which you pursue your ordinary ambitions as other men do. I did as well as I could in my schooling. I became a civil servant after leaving school. I studied in the evenings and I was very happy to be transferred to the Ministry of Foreign Affairs. There were little question marks in my head as I grew up, but finally I became a representative of a racist regime and I had the task of having to defend policies that the rest of the world knew to be oppressive and evil, but which we had been brought up to believe were just the way that life was. It was a long bitter process for me to clear from the dark corners of my mind all the residues of a very evil system that gets deep into your soul.

It was the begining of the work I'm doing now. Not because I went into it with a guilt complex or because I'm trying to atone for the past. But because it gave me a very clear insight as I struggled to understand the sources of injustice. When one tried to defend the herding of people into small pieces of land, as is being done now in the bantustans, one realised that what was being created were vast reservoirs of labour in which people were dependent on migrancy, in which they were to be controlled no longer by white police forces and the white army but by puppet soldiers, puppet police, who would shoot their own people because they had been given privileges within those boundaries, so they would stand guard. They had become the masters and the agents of this order.

I resigned, I returned to South Africa and I eventually joined what was called the Liberal Party. It believed at least in one man, one vote, and I struggled within it and ran into difficulties, harassment by the police. I went abroad and helped to promote the boycott campaign in 1960. I tried to return home and there was then an emergency and many thousands of people were arrested. I came back to a situation of great hostility for having participated in a boycott campaign abroad. I was considered a traitor and I went underground and wasn't discovered. But the Liberals felt that it was dangerous to try to hide me and they took me to Swaziland; hence this long process of exile of nearly twenty-two years began.

I went to Bechuanaland, as it was then in 1962, because I didn't like living the life of a political exile, and began this work of education. Not having any special experience of education or qualifications as a educator, it was simply a recognition that education, as I saw it then, was a necessary tool of development. The Bechuanaland of those days had six secondary schools and something like fifteen per cent of those who left primary school went on to secondary school. For the rest there was nothing to do. So it seemed then that what one ought to do, if possible, was to try to create in those people, who were fortunate enough to get an education, a sense of responsibility for the development of the society as a whole, and we tried to introduce measures into our secondary schools to achieve this.

First of all, we evolved a course in development studies which was an attempt to analyse social development historically, and in countries like Botswana; to present choices and options that people could take, also to give them skills, practical skills in building, and to involve them in the building of their own school. We had quite a lot of success, and managed to develop three secondary schools. The initial response and participation of people in those schools was very encouraging to us, because the more response we had, the more we were able to contribute to that process ourselves.

But over the years we had a certain resistance: the young people felt that the courses which we were offering were taking time from the conventional courses they would need to pass their examinations. They resented the involvement in the voluntary labour with which we were constructing the school. We had in the meantime initiated another programme, something we called the 'Brigades', because we recognised that the problems we were dealing with were economic. There were not the resources to train and educate everybody who wanted schooling, and the extent to which we could involve people in the building of their own school or running of the school, in providing their own food, in making their own equipment, their own furniture, the extent to which we could do that, was the extent to which we saved resources and were able to use the resources we saved for expansion. The Brigades built on this principle, by producing goods and services which yielded a considerable amount of money, enabling us to pay teachers, to pay instructors, in other words, to develop a model which involved people's participation in their education and training.

We did encounter many difficulties. We had many strikes by the students in these different types of programmes, resentment of the time spent in this work, resentment of the fact that the food which they received was not as good as in the main system. In other words, we had the main system, the ordinary system of education, and we were trying to develop an alternative. The problem about the main system was that it used the scarce resources of poor countries to give a very high standard of education to a few, at the neglect of the great majority. This great majority could only be mobilised through their own activity, and they became resentful because they compared themselves with those who were better off.

We tried with our development studies to equip people with an analysis, so they could say, 'We understand the workings of the society; we see this is why it is; we will become critical of the formal systems of the society'. The problem then became political, because here was a confrontation between the alternative and the main system. It led me to make an analysis of the formal systems of education, and to withdraw from the secondary school which I had started, to concentrate my energies on the development of the Brigades as an alternative to try to increase production.

Again we encountered the problems that emerged from the way that society developed as a whole. In the early days, Botswana seemed to be a very poor, arid country, dependent on cattle, and from the government there was some support for our system because it also helped them to solve their problems. But in the late sixties and early seventies mineral developments began to take place. The country was richer than we thought, and the resources enabled a much better concentration on the formal systems, but still to the neglect of the great majority. The great majority were still not going to school and couldn't find work.

What I'm trying to stress is that the alternatives are absolutely essential in the Third World, to the training of people and the provision of work. We are all locked into an international economic order in which the people who rule in the industrialised world and those who rule in the the Third World are in a sense accomplices and rivals. But we in the Third World are part of the system in which resources are exploited, in which we have monoculture, the culture of one crop economies. These are exported, and enclaves are created in each of these countries in order to support exports to the industrialised countries and imports into the Third World countries. Supporting these enclaves are the educational systems, mainly designed to train people for the civil service or people who are able to find high level technical jobs in the industries.

The alternative must do something else. It must be able to make people creative, not simply work seekers within the enclave economies. It must enable them to develop with their own skills and energies the agricultural resources of the country. It must enable them to take part in small-scale industrial development, it must enable them to use alternative technology, to develop systems and models of development which mobilise people on their own, in a self-reliant way, into satisfying first of all the basic needs and then from there on to produce for the satisfaction of other needs.

We need, for instance, an educational system that is linked fully into society and all its activities, recognising that education is not a separate category which takes place in schools, which is highly verbalised, very theoretical, very abstract in its measures, but that it is linked up to all other development. I think that was the key lesson that I learned in the early days of this schooling: that the best way of learning is to involve people in the real activities which underlie all the concepts they are learning about.

The lessons I learned in South Africa, the rejection of

racism, a dedication to opposing racism, remains always with me. But having lived in Botswana I have discovered that there are injustices perpetrated also within nations and races that have nothing to do with racism itself, and I have come to see that there are deeper underlying social causes. It isn't possible to say that we would like to have some more benign form of capitalism in South Africa, free of racism, because in that manifestation of capitalism, racism is actually inherent. The whole system of migrant labour is built upon exploitation of people.

The creation of the bantustans wasn't only an act of the racist, but began with a need of the mines and the farms to have cheap labour totally at its mercy, which it could regulate, while the wives and children were kept in the reserves so that they would have to feed themselves there. Their employer didn't even accept that obligation. He simply fed the men and paid them enough to survive on, and they returned at the end of the contract to ensure that they never thought that they would belong to the place where they worked, but their homes lay somewhere else.

Our work in Botswana has had its ups and downs. We have at least developed educational alternatives which in one place, the place where I worked in Serowe, trained 400 young people in thirty-five different skills. We produced milk and eggs and vegetables, we were able to produce cooking oil, we built houses, we could repair engines, we were able to produce clothes and we had printing presses. There was a wide range of activities which meant that the young people were engaged in a process of development which also changed them, and was an essential part of their education.

We see the process of linking education with production as a part of the whole process of social, economic and political development itself. It is essential that, in moving away from other models of development, from copies that are taken straight from the industrial societies, that we should give people the where-with-all to understand the problems of their society and to be able to do something about them. I feel that this kind of development is important, not only to the Third World. As we see in the industrialised world more and more young people unemployed (in Britain half the school-leavers now cannot find work), we recognise that the solutions to these problems lie within education as much as they lie within society.